PTSD

Road to Recovery

One Soldiers
Story

Bob Bray

Second Edition

Disclaimer

In other words, PLEASE don't steal our stuff. We worked hard to prepare it. Plus, the Dynamic Discovery program is all about honesty and stealing is just wrong.

Limits of Liability/Disclaimer of Warranty

This material is designed for educational purposes only. The author takes no responsibility for any misappropriation of the contents stated in this e-book and thus cannot and will not be held liable for any damages incurred because of it. While the author of this book has made utmost efforts to obtain updated and accurate information contained herein, the author and/or the publisher of the book cannot be held liable for any damage or loss caused by the content of this book. The author of the book does not warranty the accuracy of the contents and disclaims all warranties with respect to the information contained herein, its accuracy and applications.

The advice presented in this book may not be suitable for everyone. The information contained herein is not intended to substitute for informed medical advice or training. This book is not a substitute for professional advice and the information in this e-book should not be used to diagnose or treat a health problem. Dynamic Discovery is a process of self-evaluation. Neither the author nor the publisher of this book is engaged in rendering any professional services. If expert assistance and guidance is needed, professional help should be sought.

The author of the e-book does not endorse any person whose quotations have been used in this book. Neither the author nor the publisher of the book takes any credit for the cited quotations.

Individual results may vary.

Other Books By Bob Bray

PTSD Road to Recovery Workbook

Attention Deficit Disorder in Adults

Attention Deficit Disorder in Adults Workbook

The Complete Guide to Attention Deficit Disorder in Adults

Trauma and Recovery Guide for Victims of
Sexual Abuse Workbook

My Life with PTSD and ADHD (Collection of Cartoons)

Contents

FOREWORD

When I heard Bob's stories about his experiences with traumatic incidents, I encouraged him to write them down. I believe that Bob has a firm grasp on what it's like to experience Post-Traumatic Stress Disorder (PTSD), and he also knows what one has to do to overcoming trauma of the condition.

I have used the word "condition" deliberately, simply because the cause and effects have been known for a long time under different names. Let me explain.

As I understand it, Post-Traumatic Stress Disorder, or PTSD, is a new name for a very old condition. In the earlier 1900s, it was known as "shell shock" or "battle fatigue." Before then, it had no name. One definition says that PTSD occurs when a witness or victim of a terrible event or tragedy is so haunted by memories of the event that personal health and personality is affected.

In this book, Bob makes it easy to relate to PTSD through his story-telling approach – and it is always easier to read a story rather than suffer through a lecture.

While there is lots of research on the topic, there is not a lot of effective treatment that is readily available for most of those people who are affected – which makes this book timely and a good read for those who need to know more about the signs, symptoms, effects, and treatment of Post-Traumatic Stress Disorder.

- by George Bissett

The cartoons in this book are not intended to offend or minimalize the important issue that is Post Traumatic Stress Disorder. It is an interpretation from my own personal experiences.

"If we couldn't laugh, we would all go insane."

Robert Frost

Introduction (important)

I LIKE WHAT George has to say about Post Traumatic Stress Disorder (PTSD). When I relate to my incident(s) of someone who needed help with PTSD, I see how it unfolded to become what it was for me as a soldier, a policeman, a person. I initially wanted to get the book and workbook out there and put out my basic story. I have since amended it to include more information about all the idiosyncrasies I believe are involved in such a complicated trauma therapy. I by no means have all the answers and at the conclusion I have asked for your stories, which can help refine my information.

I see PTSD as a very complicated trauma with many unusual behaviors, many of which are entangled and further complicated by many painful memories and equally complicated treatment programs. I do believe it can be reasonably healed. The use of our strategies to cope, manage and deal with it will provide the sufferer with relief and a respite from this twisted life of torment, which destroys our families and us. By diligently working through our workbook, excellent results can be obtained.

As part of our desire to continually make our programs even more effective, we will be releasing an online version. I expect our online program by Christmas 2015.

I want to provide some background, as I believe our life before our incident, whether PTSD or a Critical Incident, sets the stage for us to develop the syndrome. I speak to what I believe are the causes of PTSD.

I find many sufferers start with ADD or Co-dependency, which arise from either birth or upbringing, schooling, and coping mechanisms we learn on our own. I speak of co-dependency and how it affected me as well as being ADD/ADHD. I have a friend who came from a family of good straight people. He was raised well without my past but began drinking at eight years of age to calm his ADD (tested positive). It turned out grandpa was a big drinker (ADD can be inherited). You can have the ADD brain and suffer some abuse in one form or another, but you still have it. It just gets a little trickier when it comes to repairing the damage. As you now have PTSD, co-dependency, abuse, addiction, and maybe another Critical Incident, and you can't get it out of your mind.

There is also an area of concern called Reactive Attachment Disorder (RAD), which shows up in many people displaying signs of ADD/ADHD. Consideration is because of the inability for the child to form an attachment with primary caregiver probably cause the caregiver doesn't care or suffers from serious depression, addiction, bad relationship, etc. All the child seeks at this age is love and nurturing. If this does not occur in meaningful manner, the child will not form proper attachment to the caregiver (RAD). The first year is crucial.

RAD can begin during gestation when mother is exposed to additional stress other that usual pregnancy. This can be domestic disputes, violence, and chemical abuse, homeless with children. Another consideration is if the mother has been raised in a similar fashion where she does not receive the proper love and nurture, she will pass on these lessons to the child. What I mean here is a lack of holding, responding to the child's unanswered cries for attention for food, changing and love. This form of lack of caring will produce considerable more damage if carried on until the age of four. This can apply to the father not caring or paying attention as well but not as crucial in the first year. There can also be a concern for an absence of either parent for learning proper sex role. This can be from abandonment or just by absence for the preference of drinking, drugging, military absence, suicide, etc. The child can grow with the belief of actually being abandon.

RAD can also apply to the child being exposed to violence, heated arguments and of course violence being applied to the child. We don't forget, we just bury it very deep but it is there to haunt us later in life if we are exposed to more traumas. We only need look at the Eastern European children dropped in orphanages at birth and see the making of cold uncaring persons, some to become psychopaths.

We will compound the problem with military training or police training and working the job in a subculture that further compounds the training. Now we have a soldier who for sure is hyper-vigilant, which is great for combat, and now we return him/her to civilian life but he now has anxiety (same as hypervigilance). A person needs to be released from the PTSD trauma, but also from all the other crap in their life. It can be done, but not overnight. The ethical part is this isn't the military's problem. They didn't create the past for the soldier, but they furthered it with the training and the lifestyle. There is some degree of co-dependence created when you train somebody to rely on higher ranks to feed you, clothe you, provide your bed and safety, and tell you what to do. And one day, they kick you out, especially if you've become a behavioral problem

We will compound the problem with military training or police training and working the job in a subculture that further compounds the training. Now we have a soldier who for sure is hyper-vigilant, which is great for combat, and now we return him/her to civilian life but he now has anxiety (same as hypervigilance). A person needs to be released from the PTSD trauma, but also from all the other crap in their life. It can be done, but not overnight. The ethical part is this isn't the military's problem. They didn't create the past for the soldier, but they furthered it with the training and the lifestyle. There is some degree of co-dependence created when you train somebody to rely on higher ranks to feed you, clothe you, provide your bed and safety, and tell you what to do. And one day, they kick you out, especially if you've become a behavioral problem.

I'm not sure how others experience flashbacks, but I have experienced flashbacks in my life from some of the more painful experiences. The experience seems to be happening all over again, just like I was right there in an associated state. I felt everything (tactile), saw everything, heard everything, and felt the emotion. It captured me for the moment. I don't get these anymore unless it is an experience newly surfaced, but now I know how to deal with them to remove the emotion from the memory. The worst part, other than reliving the experience, would be the weird mood I would be in afterwards. I would be aggressive, or even hyper-alert to whatever was going on around me, almost like I wanted to hurt someone and then depression sets in.

I'll tell you one soldier's story from my perspective and when, I believe, I got screwed up. And I'll narrate the way we behave and what we look like. I have tried to look at the world in what we do to others and finally what we can do to make changes. I see the challenges as being visible to everyone else but ourselves. Once we can become aware of ourselves and how we behave, we might need to find help and a plan to change ourselves.

I want to speak a little about some important terms; these are the short form of definitions that I will use throughout the book. Epinephrine or Adrenalin is considered the anger hormone. It prepares our body for fight or flight. It is the energy behind most of our emotional states – fear, anger, anxiety, joy, and jealousy. Anger is produced by a combination of Epinephrine and Norepinephrine (Noradrenalin). Together these provide the "feeling" of a feeling, the tingle, excitement, and energy. These two act upon all of our body organs like stimulating the heart, constricting blood vessels in order to use blood where it is required for emergency use. We can use these combinations to learn, for memory, ability to concentrate; performance can be improved to a point. If the body is flooded with these chemicals, rational thinking, concentration and performance decline. Reaction or reflex training runs things at this point. Dopamine plays a major role in reward-motivated behavior within us. Whatever we might decide is a reward, we will at some point in our life, produce dopamine as needed. If we decide we really like something or like looking at something, our brain will produce dopamine. Porn might be an example for some just as driving fast for might be for someone else.

Apparently we all have an ego. It is a cunning part of us that can split in two in that it can endorse good or bad. I believe that some of us have the ability to function as two or more people at times. We can be this family person who isn't very good at it but goes to church and makes some effort at being a good employee, neighbor and perhaps friend. The other side of this guy is anyone but the person I just described. He might have some addiction problems to sex, drugs and rock and roll. He probably has some road rage, a short fuse, a girlfriend, and possibly porn issues, likes to drink (or use other substances), and has periods where he will try to control all around him. At times he may feel like he is losing his mind because he is tormented by memories or behaviors, he has no control over.

This is a book about change and how to go about it. There was a character called George Costanza on a show called Seinfeld. His life was in the toilet continually until he started doing everything the opposite from the way he thought he should do it. I began doing many things the opposite way I thought I should and my life got better.

Chapter One

I CAN STILL remember my first spanking, which in retrospect seems to be a bit excessive for a three-year-old. We were on a picnic on a nice summer day in a park-like area. I was wearing a white short outfit, so it must have been mild. I found this screw top can, and I could hear something inside it when I shook it. I asked my dad to help me open it, and he told me to throw it away. I am still an inquisitive person today and was probably more so 64 years ago. I got it open and spilled some chemical on my white outfit. I wasn't very smart for a three-year-old as I was now more concerned about the mess on my clothes (I had a bit of an OCD clean thing about me as a kid, maybe today as well). I went and told my mom, and she turned me over to my dad. He was a bit crippled, and he bent over and tried to swing me over onto his knee. I escaped as I was scared, and I don't know why, maybe this wasn't the first time. He wasn't able to catch me, as he had a bad leg. I went to my mom, as I didn't know what else to do since I had no survival training at this point in my life. I didn't run off into the bush and didn't even have the thought. When my mother handed me over, she had said take it like a man. I had forgotten this incident, but this is probably where my rage came from.

A psychologist told me about six years ago that I suffered abandonment issues and betrayal plus other problems such as anger because of this. Some of my past might be buried below my conscious memory. I got a flashback of this when looking through an album about eight years ago and saw a picture of this day; grief immediately overcame me. I hadn't cried before, or even remembered this incident.

But I felt severe emotional pain and relived the entire incident. My mother had betrayed me and turned me over to a giant who beat me, and she finally stopped him physically because he wouldn't stop. He said, "I'll give you something to cry about" because I couldn't stop crying when he told me to. What I did learn that day was that I was supposed to be a man, even though I was just a little kid.

It's a good thing that there weren't standards for being a man. As I was a little short and somewhat immature, especially emotionally, which would later haunt me because I did not know how to respond when things got tough except to run away. I couldn't trust anyone, not even someone I loved, and if they said they loved you, well that was just words. I learned to not express my feelings, as that just resulted in more hurt. Don't express your feelings; angry, sad, scared, as that just gets you hurt. This became a major problem in later relationships.

I grew up in a violent type of family. I was bullied, intimidated, and beaten at times. When I was about three, my older half-brother told my mother that he wanted to cut me, and then he was removed from our home in Toronto and sent to my grandpa's in Winnipeg. I know now that this turned into a disaster for him. He never got over what he suffered being bounced from grandpa's to another unfortunate alcoholic family setting. When I was six and went to school, I was continually bullied and beaten by my brother's friends on a daily basis. My brother was never there, but I would see him on the school bus afterward. I guess he didn't like me even more after what he had been through.

All I was ever able to do was hide somewhere and cry and get angry, as anger would get me away from the feeling of sadness. I later learned that my brain produced adrenalin to get me out of my depression (sadness).

One time, when I was eight years old, and we had been working in one of the fields, my older brother was picking on me, and I snapped and chased him back to the farm with a paring knife and tried to stab him. Luckily, I didn't catch him. I wanted to kill him. However, he didn't pick on me for a long time after that. That type of response indicates a lot of rage for an eight-year-old. Of course, there had been other beatings from my dad after the first one I remembered, but that was becoming my "normal."

I think I was pretty good at turning off my emotions. That is where emotional maturity gets stuck, and you become unable to determine what you need to feel when something occurs, especially in the adult world. My brother died last year, but earlier in the year I had been able to let go of my anger towards him and put this behind me. I saw him about a week before he died, and I was happy that our relationship had resolved, but I regret that we missed out on so much of the brotherly affection we could have had. But we were able to spend a couple of hours together and interact as though that nasty stuff had never happened.

So as a kid I had some setbacks but don't we all? My friend George taught me that we have to learn to play the cards we are dealt, or we will make ourselves crazy.

While I was going to school, I was found to be disruptive by fidgeting, interrupting, having trouble focusing, and generally not paying attention, etc. School was a disaster for me, and probably no picnic for the teachers as well since they were unable to motivate me. I was labeled incorrigible. I was given some tests when I was about fifteen, and this one teacher suggested that I should probably join the army, as school wasn't for me. I wondered why they couldn't have tested me sooner and saved me the trouble of going to school all those years. Needless to say, I failed that year as well. For years, I thought I was stupid and wondered why I couldn't learn.

When I was eleven, an older boy who was sixteen and really big tricked me into going with him, he did stuff to me, but there was no way I was doing what he wanted me to do. He threatened to hurt me if I told anyone, when you're eleven, you believe your neighbors. For some reason, I didn't tell. How come we don't tell? Is it because we believe we are partly at fault? I worried for years that I might be a homosexual. I didn't know that you don't catch it from that kind of interaction, but I still did things to prove to myself that I was normal. I think that many of us appear as victims to predators because of our co-dependent type of personality. We can be like a deer in the headlights because we can certainly be easily intimidated into following orders. Why are strangers able to coerce children into getting into their cars - we do as we are told.

I recall having some anger issues and used to get into fights. Mostly I was on the wrong side as I lost a lot. I smoked, and it felt good and helped me relax, plus it works on some forms of ADHD. I started when I was twelve, but experimented before that. I drank the odd time as a teenager, but only got drunk once when I was sixteen. I was more interested in girls. I was still having anger issues, mostly road rage, and still got into fights, usually when provoked. I started winning more, as I would lose it and try to maim or annihilate the other person.

I had many jobs, as I would get bored. I could be very impulsive and perhaps steal from an employer or be convinced by myself, I should do this or that. I could be easily led if someone could convince me of something. I joined the army at twenty-two and spent four years as a soldier. I drank too much only twice and nearly got shot while I was in Cyprus at a Turkish outpost when my buddy (who was drunk) got very demanding about getting his cigarette lit. When the sentry chambered a round into a automatic weapon, I knew that we were in trouble.

When I was nearing the end of my service, I was a radio operator, and I worked in a command center. My job involved receiving and sending coded messages, receiving voice messages, and forwarding them as necessary, as well as sending messages. In those days, no names were utilized, and voice traffic was limited, which to most people would seem garbled. This was a major exercise involving a Regiment (three battalions). I was one of the radio operators on duty that morning, and a message came over the air to my company commander, asking had the Padre reached call sign Bray's location. I was unsure what to do, as we did not use actual names over the radio, and that is my name. My company commander answered from his radio, "no."

I remained on the radio, but questions were rampant in my head as the padre only came to see you in the event of a death in the family. I thought maybe it was my dad, as he'd had a heart attack a few months back. I'm not sure how much longer I was on the radio, but then I was in the middle of receiving a coded message, and decoding it when I was relieved of my position without explanation. As I was waiting for the Padre, I started to think, and maybe not clearly. I knew no one else in the battalion was named Bray, that maybe I had screwed up, and that was why I was relieved of my post. I was the only one in the command post on that frequency. I left the command post and sat under a tree for an hour or two as I didn't know what else to do. I could probably pick out the tree today if it's in the same place. Fortunately, it was a nice summer day. There were only a handful of us there but nobody spoke to me, and I can guess that nobody had any idea what to say. What do you say to a guy who has death coming to see him? I was reminiscing about my dad, and I thought that it was too bad I didn't get to see him before I left this last time. I thought I would be okay, but I was worried about my mom.

We were dug in when the Padre showed up. It must have been about six hours later as the light wasn't very bright. When the padre came into the heavy bush cover where we were hunkered down, he climbed down into the trench and said my three and a half-month-old son had died of crib death. I didn't know what that was. I jumped up from where we were and began running as fast as I could. I had no idea where I was going, but I guess I was still trying to run away from pain from early years. I was tackled by two soldiers and held until a syringe could be administered to me. I have no idea what they shot into me, but I had no recollection from that point until I awoke several hours later in a vehicle heading towards the base in Calgary. I fell back asleep and was woken up in Calgary.

I was assigned a bed in a barracks and told where it was. There was no one else in the building. I was trained to survive anywhere, but I just didn't care. I thought I should phone my wife, but there was no phone, and I just wanted to lie down and preferably die. I didn't know where to go to eat, so I went to bed and waited out the next morning for instructions as to where to go. I didn't sleep much, but

I knew I was flying to Winnipeg at some point. I took one of those pills. I didn't feel anything at all. Then I showered and, dressed in my dirty combat clothing and laid down and slept fitfully. Somebody came and got me, and took me to the civilian airport, but I don't remember much, just getting on the plane. And that the stewardess in first class fussed over me and brought me food and pop; apparently she knew about my loss.

We didn't go out much in public in those days in combat dress, so I got a lot of funny looks. My gear had not yet reached my location where we were dug in, and I had nothing but the gear I had on. My wife and my in-laws picked me up and took me to their place. My father-in-law gave me about eight fingers of whiskey in a glass and said drink up, you need this. Sadly, he was an alcoholic, but was not the stereotype as he had a good job, was likable, and went to church. Whenever my glass was empty, whatever time of day, he would refill it and of course drink with me. I recall meeting with my family at some point, but by now I was either drunk or stoned, and maybe both. This lasted for almost two weeks. The low point in all of this was that I missed my son's funeral because I was drunk and stoned. I didn't want anything to do with my wife, and I told her I wasn't ready for what was to come. I so missed my baby; I had given my notice earlier to get out of the army so I could get a job and be home with him. I loved him so much.

The drinking and the refilling of my glass and the pills were getting to be too much, so I made a decision to stop. My wife and I had to return home, and, because the army had given me only two weeks off, I had to prepare to get back to work. When I returned to duty, I ran into the guy I had driven (I was co-driver) with to Wainwright. He was telling a guy how I flipped out when the Padre came and told me about my son. I asked why he was telling shit like that, and he told me to fuck off; I felt rage and wanted to kill him. Too many people around to do anything but get locked up, but I plotted in my head about killing that bastard for years.

There were other incidents in my life after this one, but I was able to bury them pretty deep. I believe I became void of any and all emotions about this time. I had been attending university classes in the evenings, and it was a real challenge before this. I failed both classes I had been taking, as I was away for six weeks on exercise and then another two weeks when my son passed away. The year before, I barely passed the classes I was taking after I developed a bleeding ulcer and was hospitalized. Who knew that being anxious about passing classes, being loaded with homework, raising a family, and ongoing military training would cause a bleeding ulcer? Plus, I had been recommended for officer training, and I could not fathom how I was going to do all this. I know where the anxiety comes from today, it just sort of fit with my struggles in school. I put myself in jeopardy because I didn't want to be stupid anymore, even though being stupid was never the problem; it was the ADD… probably a bit of PTSD from the trauma I experienced and didn't do, or know how to do, anything about. Who even knew about such a thing?

You watch that side and I'll watch this side. Wake me if someone comes.

The issue becomes "Where did this anxiety come from?" How could simple things like my experiences give me ulcers? I thought back to when I was in Cyprus; I had been contacted by our rear party and told that my wife was having issues with a soldier threatening her or something like that. I had an army buddy back there, but he heard nothing. There were some issues at home with my wife, and also with my family, but everybody was reluctant to talk. My younger sister was forced to move out of my wife's place by my family. It was such a helpless feeling to be ten thousand miles away and only being able to phone my wife once a week when I went into town. It's hard to sort out problems from that far away. I didn't find out until much later that there were no threats from army guys about harming my wife. There was another issue, but no one was harmed except me in that story.

I tortured myself by wondering whether I would become like my mom. My mom was kind of crazy. She could switch like Jekyll and Hyde in a millisecond. She suffered much abuse as a child. Once, she jumped from a car at fifty miles per hour, which turned out to be a really bad move. I worried about what would happen if I lost another child. I didn't want to have any more children, as the mere thought was too painful. What was happening to my marriage? I get it now; I might have been dealt that anxiety problem, but how did it get so out of hand? All the problems I faced were possible problems in the future. Nowadays we call that anxiety.

I see this anxiety stuff as a result of training or conditioning or self-conditioning where the person who has been able to extend their training through this additional exposure becomes somewhat, or totally, apathetic. This is similar to where the military creates a vigilance within us to be alert on sentry post, because if a boogeyman sneaks up on us we'd all be dead, so now you become vigilant. Some of us, especially if in combat, can turn this into hyper-vigilance based on our normal anxiety level vigilance. So instead of just remaining awake during sentry duty, we are really alert and see everything and hear everything all the time even in our sleep. The problem becomes, how do we turn it off when we leave the military?

We are conditioned by many ideas in the military, and sometimes recruit trainers might lack consistency on how the book might be followed. The person in charge of one barrack block might have higher standards than other barracks commanders, and the punishments might be tougher with more discipline. I recall going through basic training, and then infantry training in a different location with different instructors, but they always seemed to focus on the weaker guys, or guys more prone to making mistakes. I watched instructors scream, abuse, and belittle some of the recruits. Perhaps some of these guys didn't catch on as fast as some of the others, let alone the quick learners. They might be subject to public ridicule. Some of these instructors picked on some of us continually. I had been selected as a course leader in our barracks and handled delegating tasks for cleanup and marching our platoon from one location to another. This one instructor seemed to dislike me and would call me a little kiss ass and make me do pushups until I couldn't do anymore. I could do seventy-five either clap or knuckle push-ups by the end of basic. I remember some of these guys would cry at night, or even sometimes on the parade square. That sadness is sometimes referred to as depression, and for some it would last for six months and feel like punishment. I wonder how hard it was for those guys who had problems to begin with, and then were tormented by other recruits as well as instructors. Some dropped out, but most stayed. I wonder if there was just no place to go for some peace. It was sort of like the first place many of us fit. When I look back and wonder at how many people had ADD when I was in the military, I think there were lots. And lots of them didn't finish high school in those days. I don't think much has changed because grade 12 is a giveaway today because you just get pushed through. It's almost like a default setting; you just have to put in time. There is also the grade 12 equivalency. So you can still get in the army, the standards haven't kept the ADD people out, especially the milder cases, and I saw extreme cases stay. Not many got pushed out, some left. You learned to cope; it was a tough job even if you fit in - but even there, the bullies picked on the weaker ones.

Let's take a look at the military training concept. Some have likened it to a form of brainwashing. We change our clothes to wear a uniform; we have many different uniforms, but we always look the same. We cut our hair or wear it the same as the others. We change the shape of our bodies through physical fitness. We learn history and military law and learn to behave the same way. We learn to function as a team through drill and to move around the base as a team together, always marching or jogging. We eat, sleep, and spend twenty fours a day together for months at a time. We spend our off time together if we ever get any. We make our beds the same; we learn to clean up our quarters together. We even sort of like the people we don't like; isn't that crazy? We spend a lot of our time learning how to shoot at man-shaped targets. Then we learn how to shoot at man-shaped targets hidden in the bush that jumps up at you to help us react quickly to sudden movement by shooting quickly. There is no discerning, just shooting.

During infantry training, I was issued a fully auto weapon. I provided live fire for my platoon to learn how to move under. The better you get, the better soldier you become. Let's face it, this isn't about babysitting, it's about killing. You know by now that this is about staying alive under fire. You develop close ties with your buddies, as the bonds become about who will look after you if times get tough. No one gets left behind. Your mother might be the only one who would risk their life for you except your army buddies. We aren't aware, but we are also learning about apathy after awhile. It becomes us against them, and them becomes anybody who is not your buddy; other soldiers, other military, and so on down the line. A loved one may find themselves lower on the list in a category called civilians. Watch what happens in a bar fight with military people, we would even side with the navy in a fight with civilians.

In last place is the enemy, which are the targets you shoot at or bayonet and you build up goals to do your job, but never get to achieve this until one day something bad happens. All this produces some good adrenalin but no outlet, which produces some downtime after the adrenalin rush, addicting, yes. If you wonder why infantry guys don't make good peacekeepers, it's because they are trained to kill not to coddle. I also believe there is some degree of frustration involved in this whole peacekeeping idea, and the Canadian Military was on top of it.

When we sent soldiers to Somalia, we sent the Airborne Regiment; our crack troops. These guys are trained to do everything the infantry does, but even better thanks to their extreme training. But their main job is to kill and in so many different ways. They also learn how to interrogate and get the truth quickly out of suspects. Sound like versatile guys, right? This job is like so many jobs, we train people to do a job a certain way, and then we frustrate the hell out of them by not letting them do it. These guys get the job of babysitting a country that has an enemy they can't tell from the good guys. So all this reactive training that you know how to respond to doesn't fit in your head. What do you do now? So we get into a situation where we are called upon to do our job, and we become what we are trained to do. We react according to our training. Going sideways in your head is an example of how it can go wrong. The solution was to put a couple of soldiers in jail and disband a proud regiment and its history. Sort of makes sense to me, what else would a person do? Almost sounds like the military (or the civil service) got a politician to help them make a typical political decision. Get rid of the perceived problem, find some scapegoats, and don't let anything stick to high-ranking officers - especially those generals who make ridiculous decisions like this in the first place. And all because some politician decided that, since we've got all these trained killer soldiers sitting around; waiting for something to do, let's give them a mission.

As soldiers, we just do as we're told. Decision-making becomes not so important because you have come to rely on somebody to feed and clothe you, look after your well-being. And in return all you have to do is obey orders and you will be reasonably safe. Especially if you are overseas or in a different part of your country, you have to do somewhat as you are told. It is easy because, at the end of your training, you have become fairly reactive, but now you are even better at taking orders and following through with them. You now get to play with the big boys, and the peer pressure is on to act like they do. It's either handle the pressure or be crushed by it. It's almost like a union; seniority means a lot.

A big part of the problem is when you leave, or when you have another focus in your life, such as wife, kids, and civilian friends, or when you leave the military. You have all this hyper vigilance going on in you, and you may have flashbacks because you are always looking around and watching for the bad guys. (Flashbacks are actually reliving the scene in your mind, complete with all sights, sounds, tactile, and emotions, which occurred in the actual scene; so that you actually believe that you are back there). Who are the bad guys? Are they the ones we learn about in the army, the part of the "they" which was almost anybody other than our buddies, the hodgees, the gooks, maybe even civilians? How on earth do we turn all the army skills we learned into civilian jobs? We return home as trained killers, but there is no easy turn-off switch from being a trained killer to a normal civilian. As I said before, this is a brainwash job that soldiers and cops then get to live within the subculture that reinforces the training.

I recall attending the employment center after leaving the military, and the lady wanted to know what my training specialty was. I told her mostly weapons, light vehicles, and radio operator. She said everybody learns a trade, what was yours. I replied; infantry mostly search and destroy. She was fairly certain that I was stupid, as she persisted in asking, what was my trade? I figured it was like the army; some people were just not promotable. I also said to myself, "Stupid f-ing civilians" and wondered afterward, "Do I hate all civilians?"

I spoke of the names we come up for people to depersonalize them. Racial profiling nicknames are frowned upon in training and overlooked during operations, but are coping mechanisms to help us kill the enemy. If we can de-humanize them, it becomes easier to perform our jobs. It is often hard to treat people in a hard non-human like fashion or even kill them if we have to. It becomes easier if we cease to see them as people and provide a generalized stereotypical name. It is certainly much easier to live with hurting or killing an innocent if they are no longer human. Besides, they don't want us there.

I left the military to become a policeman, and so I had to go back to school and try to learn and study and pass exams and worry about passing. We moved to another city and bought a house. Initially, I had some problems finding employment (ex-soldiers are not well regarded at times) until I was able to apply for the police. My wife was pregnant, and the pay wasn't going to be much, and I wondered whether we would be able to survive. There was definitely some anxiety going on. And the marriage wasn't working out. It was a struggle after losing a baby, and I was having flashbacks of when the padre told me about the baby and some memories of the problems when I was overseas.

This policing was a drinking culture, and drinking soon became something I was interested in doing. The drinking helped me to get along with my wife, mostly because I wasn't home. And then, I became interested in other women. When I look back, it seemed to be a certain type of woman, one of co-dependence nature because they were so easy to talk to and get to know. They were very sympathetic to my failing marriage to a woman who didn't understand me. It was almost like an addiction, and when I drank, there was sure to be a woman nearby. I knew I was getting kind of crazy and knew I had to change.

One time, I was driving home from a party, and almost hit a pole. From that point on, I had decided to clean up my act and started training for a marathon. I became serious about training, maybe a little too serious, because I was getting a high from running. Who knew that fitness could also be addicting? Anything we do which becomes an obsession, or we extract some form of high from, might be an addiction.

I had been a policeman for a few years probably seven or eight when a guy robbed a store with a big knife to get a ham early in the morning. I guess when you are high, you get a little hungry. I was on the scene fairly quickly and took the store clerk with me to cruise the area. We came across the suspect. I approached him with my revolver drawn; he pulled out a knife, which was fairly big with a blade ten to twelve inches. He began advancing towards me, and I shouted, "Halt! Police." He continued to advance, and I drew a bead on him. Suddenly, all I saw was a police target resembling the darkened silhouette of a man (police training target). He had ceased to be a person. Everything turned into slow motion as he advanced towards me, and I could see the hammer pulling backward towards me as I pulled the trigger with my finger. I warned him again. I could hear sirens in the distance; I later found out that the store clerk had pressed the emergency button on my police car radio. I had told him to stay in the car and press the emergency button if he saw I was in trouble. The sirens were about ten feet behind me, but I could barely hear them. I heard a loud metallic sound at the same time, but it too was off in the distance. He had dropped the knife, probably when he saw that other marked units had arrived, but all I saw was the target and the hammer coming further back on my weapon. Suddenly, I saw two uniformed officers in my field of view. I had been about to shoot the person who was now unarmed. I already knew in my mind that I would pull the trigger twice into his chest area, it was no longer a thought, but it was like a program that was playing in my head. I guess I still felt that he was going to kill me, or I was still in reactive mode.

To compound this, my supervisor tried to have me disciplined for endangering the store clerk and not waiting for back up, as I was working alone and possibly using excessive force. It all became confusing because we found the suspect, and I had to react quickly to prevent his escape, and the clerk was safe. I had made a good arrest, no one was hurt, but now I was in trouble. I inquired about a commendation for a good arrest and was told that I wouldn't get any commendation as I was just doing the job. We had had many other issues, myself, and this supervisor. So now I got some added stress.

By the way, the guy I arrested, who was high at ten in the morning, pled guilty to armed robbery, while I was just stressed, depressed and worried about the trouble I might be in. Depression is a sadness you feel out of what may be a tense experience when the adrenalin wears off and becomes frustration (the past). The anxiety is what you feel will happen in the future, such as worrying that this would become an internal investigation - and then what will happen (fear of the future).

I am sure the supervisor wasn't working that day, and if he was, he didn't provide any backup for me. But he could certainly hindsight anything I could ever do. He ended up being transferred to the kiddie cops as he had been caught lying to me, falsifying documents, and tampering with personal evaluations (yay, justice). By then, I was sick of this phony-baloney job where someone could just screw you because they couldn't make you the kind of policeman he thought you should be (he had serious control issues). He rode me continually for a couple of years, and there was lots of stress, I can vividly remember one experience when he stopped a vehicle I had stopped after I cleared it. The guy waved me down afterward when he was getting into a cab, which I suggested, and told my partner and me this story. "Listen, I don't like cops, but this is what the guy who identified himself as your supervisor said to me." He asked me if the guy who stopped him was rude to him as he was having problems with him. He told him to fuck off. He was a big guy and fairly drunk and driving an expensive car. The supervisor caught him driving where I didn't. He must have been afraid to arrest him. So, I knew for sure he had been out to get me, soliciting complaints.

Anxiety is based on a fear of tomorrow or the future of what might happen or what we think might happen. An example might be if you thought that someone was to break into your house at night. Your reaction was to return you to a combat situation in the here-and-now, because of the sudden shock of believing that someone had entered into your anxiety or confused reality. This is where your past betrays you, and you relive the past instead of now.

I eventually met a nice lady, and we got married and had two children, but we lost one at thirteen years of age. He had been sickly since birth, and we knew months in advance that he was going to die. We thought that we were prepared, but we weren't.

When I left this job after fifteen years, and I got to take my anxiety (some call it a policeman's disease; paranoia) and depression from some of these unpleasant experiences with me when I left. She thought the job was making me crazy, nope, already there. Most of my problems had arisen from this supervisor who had gone to great lengths to help me leave. That "we/they" mentality I spoke of earlier was certainly part of the reason to go. There is no "un-training" for what you have learned to help keep you alive or even keep your job, and it becomes a part of you. You also learn to cope, to develop an attitude of apathy, maybe sometimes against the administration or higher ranks, civilian population, or bar patrons, because in most cases when you are in trouble only your cop buddies will help you. Does everybody become the enemy? Just like soldiers, the enemy and civilian population don't appreciate you like your buddies do. It's like knowing that they will come when the chips are down no matter what. The problem is that the injustice can live in you for a long time afterwards. That is the "we-they" mentality.

I had quit police work (honorably) after fifteen years as I just had enough of the bullshit and thought I could do better elsewhere.

Fast forward a few years and again my addictive behavior kicked in; I was drinking again, and it seemed pretty good when it went down. I wasn't drinking the quantity I had in the past, but it took the edge off. I picked up an attachment to porn, as I didn't have to go out to find my stimulation. My wife stayed in her office and listened to music, and I sat in the kitchen and looked at porn for a couple of hours. Who knew that just looking at porn was so addictive? My obsession started with soft porn, and then turned to hard. I didn't get it why some masturbate, I didn't, I just spent hours watching and stimulating my little reptile brain. My son was upstairs doing his homework, and I missed those opportunities to spend time with him. Who knew that we could be addicted to an overabundance of dopamine, and then suffer withdrawal when we stop? A lot of problems came to the surface at this point. I had depression, road rage, intolerance, and impatience with my wife. This marriage ended badly in the sense that we had ceased having anything to do with each other. I wasn't interested in counseling or even trying to work things out, I tried counseling and the counselor and my wife took sides and I just gave up and listened. We didn't get along anymore, and working together wasn't working out. The first marriage not only ended really badly, but ugly. This one ended and we don't speak today, except through texts and only if it has something to do with our son.

Chapter Two

WHAT DO WE look like to the outside world? We were trained to be warriors, and we lived the life of a warrior. Our weapon was handy, we were ready to do battle, hyper alert, got a bit of an adrenalin high going on and we are too busy with maybe a little more adrenalin when we enter crisis mode to think of emotions at this moment, no matter what we see and do. If we show emotion at this point, it will be a display of weakness. We are taught to shoot to kill at the man-shaped target, whether a moving target or still. Over and over, you shoot this target until it becomes a reflex action, and you do it without conscious thought. However, when you get to the time when you must pull the trigger and take a life, the question you might ask yourself afterwards is about-the moral implications of taking a life, but you won't. This wasn't the way most of were raised (to kill). And, what will this split second decision, which I had no control over, do to me for the rest of my life? We tend to be pretty good at making good and quick decisions in the field but we out of the field, we somehow become this co-dependent person who makes bad decisions, who is helpless at times or resorts to drama. Does our confidence come from the uniform and or the weapon or the adrenalin from the job? When we stop being a cop or soldier or even go home, what happens to us. Is being helpless or boozing, etc. out of control really co-dependence.

The war veterans, like the first responders back home, are faced with some additional issues of returning from a combat situation to a rear position without debriefing and then back to combat. Or return to home or work immediately after leaving combat (critical situation) without de-briefing or assistance and trying to return to somewhat of a normal life. The soldier who returns must continue fighting, as there is a need to stay alive in spite of what he might have just experienced. He cannot let his guard down to mourn the passing or maiming of a comrade or to allow himself to get over his first kill or seeing bodies rotting.

How do I get over that experience if I don't have the luxury of time or resources to repair my psyche on the go or while in battle? There is no time to assimilate the memories, to find relief and just relax. The garbage becomes buried in my mind until later. Same with cops, when all hell is breaking lose you cannot stop to debrief, and then the moment passes and you feel better. And your life resumes to fight another day, and you take your garbage home with you or bury it deep in your mind to haunt you another day.

Firstly, these guys step up to do a job that many don't want to do. And, of course, we want them to keep doing the job in spite of adversarial encounters. If they have problems, we expect them to get over it quickly so they may return to their form of the trenches. The pain and suffering that happens to our soldiers, and that they see happen to others, can be likened to the same stuff our emergency workers are involved with and see. Because we need them to get back to work, otherwise we might have to fill in for them. If they develop more serious issues, we can use peer pressure or the old know it all boss approach: "You'll get over this, I did." This is bullshit; no one knows what it is like to be anyone else. The bigger problem can come from not knowing their family history, and any deeper issues that might be involved, and then telling them, "You are making a big deal out of nothing."

In a macho world, you now have additional pressure to bury your problems or be seen as a fragile kid who doesn't belong in a tough world such as ours. I am a tough guy; I have no feelings. We learn this from the old guys and it is bullshit, but we don't know any better at the beginning. These guys are mostly drunks whom are full of apathy and have no regard for anyone else. A lot of them, but not all, are old soldiers or old cops who don't know much about anything anymore but have an opinion on everything.

We are torn when we rotate back home because we have this special close environment where everybody seems to know what to do, even when only hand signals are required. We have to leave these guys behind. We are abandoning or betraying them. Did we teach them everything they need to know to stay alive, and if someone gets hurt after we leave we ask ourselves whether we're cowards or did we betray them. We may learn even more about abandonment when our families leave us because they can't stand our behavior. The only emotion we seem to have is anger, and we show it frequently. We have learned to turn off our feelings almost completely except when we are drunk, and that isn't feelings, it's being a blathering idiot. We can't show our tears because that is weakness, and also if we started crying; we might not be able to stop. The seriousness of the abandonment or betrayal issue may have been when one of both of your folks left you at an early age, and that is what you felt. And those old feelings returned.

We also have another contributor to some of our problems, and that is the bully who seems to exist merely to torment those weaker or timid. We often laugh along with the others relieved that it is not us who is the victim. But what happens to this weaker person when they get to the end of their rope? This can maybe be more visible in the way women are sometimes treated by the macho guys who see themselves as the role models of the perfect soldier or policeman. Look at me, I have the power, and I need to run things the way I think they should be run (at home as well). Does this guy beat his wife? This type often fits the tough guy, redneck persona idea as well. An old statistic about cops was there was a divorce rate of about eighty percent. Some of this comes from drinking and/or screwing around, apathy. Does that create problems in a family? What sort of trauma does our bullied victim suffer?

You want to go out there and do the job you signed on for. You may well become a victim to your employer as your behavior may change from your inability to cope with your new and forgotten surroundings. You will be the problem, troublemaker, or maybe a liability to be gotten rid of. Of course, you will become bitter during this process but it will also impact your family and friends whom are unprepared for this change and also may have an inability to accept your change or cope with it. You probably won't get the support you need. You come back with at least some anxiety and depression. When you are suffering with full-scale depression and anxiety, how much of your normal brain do you have available to think, use and problem solve? I hazard a guess that, during major depression, you've got nothing. What is it like if you don't sleep for a couple of days? Now add depression and anxiety to the mix. Now add some serious medication or a quart of alcohol. How clear can you see the world and your family and friends?

What about the spouses and kids that have to learn to go back to sleep after our screaming or yelling during the middle of the night.. We may sleep through it as this might be within the few minutes we find sleep. We don't realize the intolerance or impatience we show during our waking hours while we try to cope with our return to normal life. The soldier who is fresh from battle is whisked home and right into the arms of his family, and how does he cope with the rapid transition to normal? How does he ignore the time he has spent in combat with the people who were willing to lay their lives down for him.. His weapon was within easy reach. The weapon is not there now, and there is sheer panic for a split second when he can't find it. He was courageous, loyal and committed to doing a job he had signed on for. Now he is back on the streets of his country without his friends and his role in protecting our world. He needed a period of adjustment, but there was no allowance for that. Now he must blend into the civilian world with his family beside him. He doesn't know how to go from being a trained killer to mister or misses nice spouse and father or mother, with tolerance, without suffering something stronger than jet lag. The family sometimes appears to be whiners and complainers. We are not used to this sort of whiny talk or backtalk. What about the trauma they suffer while you behave badly awake or asleep.

Well, we can always go the medical officer and get some medication to help us cope and adapt. That will help us block that emotional pain and store it away until it can re-group with all the other painful memories we have from the conflict or our past until we explode and lash out…or take our lives. That is another step in the codependent stairway to nowhere. We can become dependent on meds and booze. Especially if we decide to mix them, which brings us around to codependency behaviors and the type of people we become attracted to for associates and wives or girlfriends because normal people will tend to avoid us. If we are with a family, they will learn codependent behavior from us by their ability to learn from our role modeling and the behavior they must exhibit to look after us.

There is no difference whether the afflicted person is a soldier or a first responder. The police officer, firefighter or emergency worker must merely change the context whether it is from emergency call to emergency call. This worker must be prepared to either heighten their response or calm down to deal with the irate person whose neighbor parked too close to their driveway. Or the many non emergent calls.. This is the customer service component for the non-combatant who has to remain calm and administer assistance after seeing more than most people see in their whole lives. Then they get to go home at the end of the shift, wired for anything but their spouse and kids. Shifts are usually run so tight in some of these organizations–that there is no slack for going home. If you say, *"The job is too difficult, I want to go home,"* the response will be *"The team can't spare you, what if someone gets hurt because you left them short-handed?"* Who carries that? Loyalty, courage, and teamwork exist within organizations outside the military as well. The training doesn't create the same sort of camaraderie, but similarities are present.

I know of a national police force that created a program where the loyalty is to the force, not to individual members. So here no one is safe as they are all individuals and capable of turning on each other in the event of one breaking the law - from speeding to whatever. The bad concept here is individuality can create more situations where bullying is a form of power used to coerce others to do your bidding. This is becoming more apparent in the complaints coming forward of female members of these types of organizations being sexually harassed. Is it for sex, power, and control, or what? Those who are victims of sexual harassment are, sometimes, also victims of PTSD.

Do all survivors live to fight another day or do they live to be victims of the last engagement in which they were involved? The part that becomes lost to the survivor is that they survived but don't consciously acknowledge that. They believe they are victims. This is where their emotional maturity becomes stuck, and they are unable to cope or find a way out of their present state of mind, much less solve this or any problem.

I find that victims of whatever form of crisis appear very similar in presentation; they appear to be merely trying to get through today and do not see anything better in their future lives. They cannot cope with today let alone their past, whether recent or long ago. Their minds are so locked up in stress (whether depression or anxiety) that they are unable to deal with their lives. Trying to manage your life when you are unable to determine a reasonable solution to any of your problems because you cannot focus on your life is a fairly dismal state. Let's add alcohol, and/or drugs (whether prescription or recreational) and you get to bury your problems again until you want to explode. Trying to put this away afterward is a bit of a challenge. Depression is difficult enough but hyper-alertness (which is trained into us to keep us alive watching for the enemy or villains). This can turn into inwards problem such as paranoia where everyone can be the enemy or hypochondria.. I know of police officers (PTSD sufferers) who carry a gun with them everywhere they went off duty and some who carried a second gun and maybe a dagger while working, for backup. What if your primary gun failed (anxiety)? What future do these guys see for themselves or their families or do they even concern themselves with the future? Probably not.

We do not like to admit to problems such as depression or anxiety as we will be branded as weak, so we tend to self-medicate with alcohol or drugs of some sort. If we follow the abuse of chemicals, we can add another problem to what we already have and now we can be addicted as well. It adds a litany of emotional problems to what we already have on our list. It can help others determine we are unfit for our jobs. In the field, we can be heroes but if we cannot adapt or get the help we need, we are now psychotics to be weeded out. How tough we must look when our family has to see us puking our guts out, or maybe we are even too drunk to clean up after ourselves or the ranting, raving or screaming during the night.

Let's start with anger, as I know it is a common reaction amongst many of us, and I had lots. Anger is some form of learned behavior in that at some point in our lives; we found it to be a workable response to a situation. The common explanation I use when explaining how it usually unfolds to a client is like this:

At some point in our life, we were in a situation where we might have been punished or over punished for something we did or something we were accused of doing.

We could have been sent to our room or our bed-space to serve out the rest of our punishment (time out).

If this were unjust or excessive, we would have a sense of injustice even at an early age. If you are a little kid, a giant usually doles out punishment. If you are an adult, a person who outranks you within an organization usually doles out punishment. It can also be a bully within a youthful culture. In any event, even if it was a parent, it may appear as bullying while you sit in your room, feeling alone, perhaps not being allowed to play, or maybe even sitting in a corner. At early ages, we do experience sadness (depression) or maybe some anxiety awaiting more punishment when dad gets home, etc. Because we aren't too bright when we are little, we might decide to complain to ourselves about the inequities of being small or unfairly punished or perhaps not even wanting to accept punishment (spoiled). This might be considered negative thinking or thinking when you consider the inequities or how wrong it is to punish me for something I didn't do. I do recall being left alone and getting angry. Sometimes even to the point of wanting to get even maybe not by spanking them but maybe running away and leaving them to be sorry for what they did to me. The secret here is anger produces chemicals within our brains (adrenalin) which kick us into fight or flight mode. Because we are so young and not too bright, our little brains have found a solution (coping mechanism) to solving the depression problem. In turn, we will keep using it because we don't know any better than to stop using this legal, yet highly addicting, drug.

Experiential learning is that ability to learn something by experiencing something whether deliberate or not and it will become a pattern for future use. And because we don't have the insecurity yet to know we might not remember things we learn, we keep this because it works to help us cope. The army uses this experiential learning to get us to remember stuff because they know it works. We use it to turn people around; it works well.

Anger can serve us during threatening experiences, and we decide whether we want to fight or flee if threatened. Our response time to a threat or perceived threat is a fraction of a second-almost like reactive. Many times it has been found to have anxiety and anger connected within our heads for anger can trigger anxiety or anxiety can trigger anger. We know how to make it work for us even at a very early age.

If you were raised in an environment where you ended up with little or low self-esteem, you might automatically substitute anger during threatening experiences to avoid being seen as vulnerable. Many of us seem to have a sense of being treated unfairly and at some point in our lives we were singled out of a group, whether at home, at school, or in the army. And we have never been able to let it go. It usually comes from an authority person, and our trust has never been restored. It can be seen a lot in co-dependent children, as they seem to have this trait many times without physical, emotional or sexual abuse. There is a whole lot more to the whole co-dependent relationship according to Dr. Janet Wotitz, but there is a whole other mess to get into. If we find these techniques work at early ages, we may use them to manipulate, control or intimidate others. It's not a deliberate action but learned behavior that has worked at least once, and we learned it well and work it.

The problem is not anger; it becomes how we use it or misuse it. Negative self-talk helps you hold onto your anger. This is the very thing that modern day news media plays off to get you to keep coming back to their channel. The more negative, gory, and unfair stories they provide, gets you back for that little adrenalin boost. We all react differently depending on our values, training, and experiences.

- We can use anger to lash out at others and intimidate them.
- We can turn it inward and beat ourselves up.
- We can use it to speak out with firmness to increase our self-esteem.
- We can use it to correct a situation that is wrong.
- Some of us also like to create chaos in a peaceful situation. This gives us a bit of a lift if we turn it into an argument to get angry to give us a bit more adrenaline, and all this without a conscious thought because it has become something we seek without knowing we do it.

Anger is a coping mechanism for dealing with some event that threatens our body, property, self-esteem, values of what we hold near and dear or when we don't get our way.

You are the only one who can make yourself angry.

You choose how you respond to events that upset you.

What you think about the event can determine whether you become angry or not.

Your thoughts and beliefs can make you angry.

Your negative self-talk helps you hold onto your anger.

Another close offshoot to anger is revenge or resentment. We can hang onto these for many years. Revenge sometimes results from situations that might be perceived as wrongdoing, injustice, or humiliation. A common idea arose during the Vietnam War, which returning soldiers had feelings of being used or taken advantage of by their country, protesters, friends, and lovers. Those same soldiers returned from fighting a foreign war and were not fully provided with benefits, and their PTSD problems were not acknowledged and led to feelings of abandonment and rejection. We don't want to be seen as weak as we were warriors, so we fake happiness and pretend we're okay to a person's face but maybe critical behind their back. This can bring on anger when we remember the scenario, and that can lead to depression because, after we come down from our anger, we will return to depression.

Our resentments can come from the people we have wronged. We have done something to someone perhaps out of revenge for something they may have done to us. This may be part of our guilt and shame beliefs. The other thought is we see people and the way they behave and we dislike them and resent them because when we look at them and see a mirror image of the way we behave. We dislike it because we were a victim to a person like this, but yet we have become that same way in a self-controlling method for our belief.

So, if we were bullied, the best way to prevent being bullied again is to be the bully. So, if you cheat on your wife, you will probably blame her for something she did and make it her fault for you cheating and resent her. In fact, you may blame her for the whole marriage falling apart because she wanted to get pregnant this month, and you weren't quite ready. Maybe there was a discussion that you don't remember but apparently you didn't argue. Now she is pregnant, and you are mad. Hopefully, you will not punish her by getting drunk and screwing around.

When this is present in our relationship with a loved one, the relationship is destined for a difficult time because, unlike anger, which is a passing emotion, resentment is a lingering emotion, which will destroy good feelings, trust, and communication. It can lead to immediate anger by merely seeing the person for whom we hold a resentment. At times, the idea about plotting revenge can enter the person's mind. Returning to the previous relationship feelings may become extremely difficult from here. It is the beginning of the end.

We learn to sleep light or live with little or no sleep. We hear everything and our senses become extremely acute for self-preservation. If we wake up in the middle of the night screaming, we might lie about being back in combat, we can't show weakness, we have to be the hero and only losers can't handle it. We are winners, right? Well, want to be, for sure. What are we seeing that scares the shit out of us? What do we fear?

Fear is closely related to anger. One way to look at fear is the idea that if we get fearful, we might engage our anger without being aware. It becomes a reaction without conscious thought. Anger overcomes fear, and we aren't fearful but now maybe on high alert, waiting for the enemy whoever that might be at whatever age we are at. We go from fear to looking for the bad guys— we call this hypervigilance, hyper-alertness, awareness pick a word, civilians call this anxiety. We pay attention to details and everything around us if we want to stay alive.

We learn to react quickly as this also is a part of the training. We learn to do things exactly right and do them over and over. Again with the experiential learning as the military knows what we actually do with our little hands becomes a brain pattern to be retained. If we don't get it right after a given number of times, we are faced with repercussions of repeated training, embarrassment, some form of punishment or humiliation. Let's put a time limit on it as well to ensure there is more anxiety trained into these soldiers, cops, emergency responders. So we learn to do in a short span but we also develop short fuses to help us react quicker to situations. It's all about speeding up the brain to be more efficient.

We learn much in training, they teach us how to look different from others by wearing a uniform, cut our hair, and get us in good shape, which changes our body shape. We look very different. Now they teach to react without thinking, we only have to see a target in order to shoot, so we shoot then think. They teach us new rules to live by. The enemy is bad, civilians are bad, they are trying to take over our world and of course, the enemy will kill our loved ones so, we generalize what we must do. Again generalizing is another speedy short cut in our thinking. Let's add a little propaganda of what might be going on to the front line soldiers now; perhaps some atrocities or what happens to us if taken prisoner? Who better to teach this than veterans who like to tell war stories and who believe they know how to insulate these fresh minds against open-mindedness. I don't believe we can train soldiers or cops to think before they pull the trigger otherwise; they might not pull the trigger when it comes time to defend themselves. But the stories and aggressive training do help to get a little anger (adrenalin) stirred up in us.

It is like our recurring dreams, they happen, and we feel them, and they can destroy our sleep even invade our drunkenness. I know some people who do not like to sleep for fear of these dreams. The dreams can be of you reliving the event over and over as yourself or disassociated. We may wander through the house while everyone sleeps, drink, watch porn, or read for hours. Some think they think but merely replay the same thoughts over and over in their heads. This is not thinking but anxiety.

The triggers that bring on the dreams or flashbacks can be from so many different reminders; different reminders that trigger you to remember an event. We saw enough stuff in a single flash of hours that most people wouldn't see in a lifetime. I awoke suddenly hearing what I thought was a noise during the night one time and thought somebody was in the house, how they would get in and hide without me hearing them (really light sleeper), I'm not sure. I was sure it was somebody who knew I was a cop and had come to get me. I scoured the house on both levels cautiously doing proper room clearing techniques with one of my handguns and a flashlight so not to alert him in case he was somewhere else in the house. This wasn't the only time that I woke out of a dream and began the empty search. Would you think I was nuts? Probably. But did I think I was nuts? NO! I actually used to think I was normal, just maybe a bit edgy at times. I overreacted to most things, which I could explain in a split second. I was usually only wearing underwear, and I never got cold even though the heat was turned down at night, sometimes I'd be sweating. I never woke up anybody while wandering around in stealth mode. Good thing I left the army, I'd have probably been declared a section eight… but I fit in with cops. Were most of them nuts too? Or did we want to show anyone the real guy who was hurting inside, no, not today.

We were part of a really tight team, that knew how to survive, work together for the good of the team. We ate together, sleep in trenches, take cover or return fire, attack when required. We also would be willing to do anything to help each other if needed. Everybody knew what everybody was going on and what to do. Or at least everybody also knew when we didn't know what was going on. Somehow we thought this is going to be a real dog fuck, what to do?

We come back to reality and dealing with families who don't know how to communicate the same way as we did. We have been brainwashed into another world, and now we didn't get *"un-brainwashed"* back to reality. The kids seem like whiners and complainers. There is no working together, there is no team, and nobody to tell us what is going on or what to do. We have gone from a co-dependent relationship to independence, and we are struggling. If I try to command this outfit, they say I am bossy, and they are not soldiers. I have to wait until everybody else eats instead of eating my rations when I am hungry. This is crazy. How did I do this before? The door slams and I jump out of my skin and duck down.

I'm not sure where it comes from - this sense of entitlement, arrogance, or maybe just, a know it all - because I certainly don't come from wealth or from where this was tolerated. In fact, we were dirt poor as kids. I was humble as a kid but somehow misplaced it. I would suggest perhaps those resentments had some nurturing ability here. I believe this attitude comes out of the co-dependency where we think we are passed the times when we will be taken advantage of anymore. If we are raised in the midst of challenges as a child, we can develop an attitude of an unwillingness to change. We cannot succeed anywhere in the world with this attitude, but we are unaware of it or our unusual behavior. Perhaps when we were small, an event occurred with us being the center. The event may have been traumatic, and our learning from this experience was, we were unable to control even our own situations. We began trying to control situations, and other people with our behavior as that was about all we could control in our lives. The behavior was usually anger or rage, and it manifested as tantrums or acting out, maybe hit the dog or cat. It would only have to work once at this early age, and we would stay with it forever.

An example of this would have been one time my wife (second wife), and I went to a kids show at the movie theater. I was carrying my son with special needs, and she was leading my other son and carrying the popcorn and drinks. She spilled my popcorn, and I lost it on her and I didn't ever know why for the longest time. For one, I was a neat freak, and it made a hell of a mess. Who cares at a movie theater but I did. The other might be my sense of entitlement. That was my popcorn and even though it could be easily replaced, I didn't see that. All I saw was mine, and it was gone. I ruined the whole movie for myself and her and probably the kids. It's the flashback into your past that you see something is taken away from you that you thought belonged to you or possibly being punished for making a mess as a kid. But the event is a reminder of the past, and your reaction is to the past, not the actual event. The child punishment may have been a loss of whatever you had. I believe we try and protect ourselves from our childhood events in today's world by being protective of ourselves and our stuff whatever it is (popcorn). If we been behaving the army way, we believe we are safe until we come home, and everything must change, and it's very difficult and stressful when someone else introduces changes or upsets our world. Just another something I've done that I can't undo but if I pretend it never happened maybe nobody will notice.

We also have expectations or entitlement that the world owes us something for what we did. People especially our family accept us and cooperate with us even though it might be sheer stupidity on their part or maybe they are as crazy as us. When our expectations are not met, we become resentful or mean. We can personalize comments made to us as though we are sensitive but what happened to the tough guy? We like to be the center of attention but if it's not positive, we get all "poor me" inside. Our thinking has become black and white, which is less prone to thinking things through again with the quick judgments. We have so many unmet needs (we are needy) which are almost impossible for anyone to fulfill for it has to be perfect too in order please us. Some of us see ourselves as this great soldier who has some delusions of grandeur, and the world needs to meet his needs, we expect it.

Perhaps an oversimplification seen in traffic might be when someone is trying to merge into your lane either by squeezing in or signaling and trying to squeeze in. If this is happening to me and I am aggressive at the time, I might not allow this to happen and provide hand signals and or explicit words. There is also the person who signals and doesn't force the issue and shows patience. My response can be to ignore their attempts or aggression. I would suggest that if we have malice in our heart at this time and we believe we own this road and others have no right to expect anything from us, they are not going to get in until hell freezes over. It's our thoughts and actions which make us either sick or healthy. Every negative thought we produce or create is just a bit of adrenaline boost especially if we can get angry.

Many of us are seeking to satisfy our need for adrenalin and we find ways of driving fast, taking chances in many ways, cheating with a neighborhood wife.. We maybe surfing for porn for periods of time, maybe at work or behind somebody's back to make it even more risky. Was it for the sex or adrenalin? When we don't get that, our instincts will find ways but we are not available or responsible, maybe helpless, have feelings of hopelessness, lonely for who knows what. We can then find a need for drugs or booze or both. We will probably still deny there is a problem with us.

One time, my new wife was making dinner, and I was standing at the island counter watching the news but being near her and blessing her with my presence. We both had got home from work about six thirty and dinner was going to be late, but that was okay because I was patient. After about ten minutes, she asked would I mind helping with dinner. She didn't seem exactly pleased to have to ask me. I asked, "What's wrong?" She responded, "Nothing." Because of what I do, I know how to question to find out what was wrong. She replied, "I'd just like a little help sometimes without having to ask for it." I immediately went on the defensive and said, "You seemed to have it all under control." In response she said, "I would appreciate just a little help, and you were just standing there watching TV." I could see where this was going, and I was being painted the bad guy. I said, "I get breakfast ready every morning and bring it to the bedroom, and we eat while we watch the news." Her immediate response was, "Oh, that's why you do it, you expect something for what you do." I tried to think of a snappy rejoinder, but I knew I was busted. I always thought I was a good guy but better yet, the thought occurred as I know I have had it for years; if I do you a favor, you owe me something to be collected in the future. That seems to be entitlement that I can see now but not then.

When I was a young soldier, I was at my mother's house, and I went into the fridge and found a big red pitcher full of milk. I picked it up in my right hand and my mom said, "Stop drinking from the pitcher, other people use it." I brought it up to my face and chugged about half a quart of the milk before I noticed the milk was sour. Being the tough guy I was, I thought I was entitled to do what I wanted but I was entitled to fresh milk and I was annoyed with her for not making sure the milk wasn't sour. And I said so. It had nothing to do with me doing something I wasn't supposed to be doing. Her complaint was legitimate but I didn't hear her complaint about drinking from the pitcher, I just thought of myself and how I was offended for being forced to drink sour milk. Meanwhile, inside my stomach, there was sort of an ill feeling occurring. Probably some would start to rethink their cocky attitude after an incident such as this. Not me.

I had already been in a few fights about road rage by this age. A couple of young guys in a Volkswagen were driving contrary to MY driving rules. I recall being cut off. A few obscenities had been exchanged, we pulled over and I quickly walked up to the car as they appeared to want to fight. I quickly grabbed the door handle and pulled while sucker punching the driver in the face. He was faster than me and started driving off with my hand stuck in the door handle, and I was unable to extract myself while running fast beside the car. I couldn't believe he was driving away with me stuck in his door handle, what was the matter with him? Luckily they slowed up and let me pull out my hand and drove off. Boy, did I have the last laugh! Not really; I was alarmed (scared maybe) while running at a sideways angle. Did these guys not understand, I had rules for driving on these roads? I thought this was a clear violation of some rules even if I were to sucker punch someone.

My wife and I were staying at my younger brother's place in another city a while back. He asks me, "When you use the shower and if you are the last one in the morning, would you use the squeegee on the shower walls." I said, "I don't do that." He didn't say anything more. Never really considered myself a redneck but here was some proof, but I didn't get it for months. I thought he was telling me what to do, and I hated that. The world sure owed me a lot, I wasn't good at hearing about others objections or complaints but they needed to hear mine which I freely stated.

I sometimes noticed in about the first few years of my policing career that I could get into situations where I wasn't as tough as I thought I was. I was working with a guy one night and we stopped a car with a lone male driving that was about my build. I was driving so, I checked the driver. I looked back to see a car pull up behind us and now I became nervous, but a couple of younger women approached the passenger side and my not-regular partner stays to chat with these girls (turns out he knew them). So I relax and proceed to the driver of the car and I noticed he is impaired and he decides he doesn't want to get out or cooperate or anything else. I get him out but by now the fight is on and we are rolling underneath his vehicle and I am trying to hit him, as I couldn't twist him around as it was too cramped to hit him as well. I finally get him in a hammerlock and drag him out and cuffed him. As we stand up, my workmate (idiot) sees from the passenger side of our vehicle what's happening on the street side and comes over and says, "What happened?" I respond, "Thanks a lot. Silly me, I thought, you would have my back," followed by f---ing a--hole. I might have said at the outset, *do your job* but I thought I could handle this (big shot). Was this a sense of entitlement? So was that cockiness or a sense of entitlement that this guy would cooperate or the other cop would do his job as I would (my rules again) that my workmate would have my back? This wasn't to be the only time as I did it again with another officer. I won in the end but, again, I had the same attitude, *I can handle this*, even though some street drunks can fight pretty good. This was nothing like the Army; soldiers had your back, as did most cops.

Rules were for other people, not me; I wasn't in the army anymore. But many cops have no trust in authority, justice or a sense of fairness. Everybody just wants to screw with us. We want to make it on our own because we cannot rely on people to be there for us. We don't like to take orders whether policy or commands at times. We don't especially like bossy people but that which we are. We develop or learn the we – they attitude.

I was lucky, I didn't see combat in the army except the crib death of my son but some seriously ugly stuff as a cop. One of the issues that comes up with people who have seen action is a sense of guilt, maybe from surviving when your partner is wounded or killed and you are not. There is a sense of abandonment or betrayal at times where we might feel as though we were left behind. We have other forms of abandonment and betrayal such as Dear John letters. We lose jobs. We couldn't hold onto it anyway. We lose friends and we may have family problems our families won't tell us about. I mean do your folks want to tell you your wife is unfaithful. We take all of this personally. We don't have much feeling left in us but this betrayal and abandonment we have.

Another part of some relevance is the grief. We can bury our feelings at the time of an incident, as we are unable to deal with the situation whether we are in combat or in a situation where we must keep working. This may deprive us of our ability to grieve in the future. We may lose a loved one and be unable or unwilling to express what we might want. Our feelings again are missing and another situation buried to haunt us in the future. Maybe we will just be angry and resent anyone we can blame even the one who passed. If we became stuck at an early age our coping skills are probably lacking and we don't know how to cope just bury stuff.

We learn to turn off our feelings based on how much we see either as soldiers, cops, and other emergency workers. We have seen too much and we develop something called apathy. We just don't care anymore about victims or our work. We might care more about driving fast or getting to the next fight, just the adrenalin works and not so much anymore. We almost need the shit scared out of us now to get a reaction from us. You might come home to all sorts of chaos and you are calm throughout without reaction. I was driving a marked police car in winter and we had freezing rain and roads were like a skating rink. We were coming up on a busy intersection and I was driving the speed limit (really bright) and I touched the brakes and suddenly we started going sideways while I madly pumped the brakes. We were coming into the intersection against a red light and came to a stop while traffic was going around us. My partner says to, "Do you see, you just stayed calm". I didn't get it, what else could I do. It takes a while to get any reaction from us.

We practice apathy unwittingly and unknowingly. However, we are able to fight with our spouse calmly. She's losing it and you are acting calm outside but maybe not inside. Is that because we don't care or feel about anything?

We don't show anyone our feelings, we might be afraid to be seen as weak. We can't cry, that would be losing control, and no one could respect us after that… especially ourselves. What if we started crying and couldn't stop, would that be crazy behavior? Oh yeah, we still have anger.

If we do try to talk to some people, usual advice is, get over it or don't think about it. When is the last time that someone was able to do either of those? People that say shit like that are just stupid. They couldn't do it themselves but the world is full of advice givers. Again this is that part of people telling us what to do or how to feel. We resent bossy people even though we might be one of them that has all answers.

Many of us drink and probably too much. We very much want to be in control and we believe this is the way. We want to control the world, the other drivers whom don't know how to drive as good as us. The people who don't know how to line up at the market. Our kids whom don't behave, as they should. If our wife would only have dinner ready when we get home and it should be exactly as we want it. We want to control everything, even our treatment program. That is where the drinking or drugging comes in. We think we can control our situation by using but how much are we really in control when we are stumbling drunk and have a vicious hangover the next day. If we drink enough, we lose sight of our morals, our family goals and responsibilities and probably a good deal of money that may have been allotted for other needs. Oh yeah, we are in control.

It's easier to go out and get loaded. In earlier days, I would go to bars with work buddies or parties or after shift parties. What would usually happen is I would get loaded; life was usually a lot simpler then. I could forget what I had seen at work, what was happening at home, what I remembered from my past. In my later days, I would go to the bar by myself, definitely not be as careful as I used to be.

Chapter Three - Toxic Relationships

I THOUGHT I'D write a different perspective on toxic relationships with the belief I might be able to tell PTSD suffers about the different disorders arising from this sort of illness. I see the results from where people who have Post Traumatic Stress Disorder (PTSD), Anxiety, Depression, Codependency problems, and ADD/ADHD problems. I have written about causes, treatment but never from the perspective of the victim. It would seem we end up in toxic relationships that we create.

I hear of the spousal and family abuse caused by drunkenness or victims of PTSD or perhaps people who are unable to cope with issues of anxiety and depression. In no way have I been making excuses for this form of conduct. I was a policeman for fifteen years and saw many forms of family and non-family abuse in the way of murder, serious assaults, rape, and incest. I also include many forms of physical assault and emotional abuse, which does not show. My list is not complete as it does not include threats, stalking, harassment which come in many forms. As a policeman, I attempted to provide a form of justice to the many victims. In retrospect, justice provides nothing in the way of restoring the victim to their previous way of life prior to the victimization or shitty marriage. It just provides some sort of revenge and that's really healthy. Today, I believe many of these victims suffered death, PTSD or became co-dependent themselves as they were not allowed to live their own life but in the shadow of someone who dominated them.

I told my story of what happened to me to show where we can go wrong ourselves and what it will do to us unless we decide we need to turn our lives around and I can offer a method of healing the trauma. I understand what a victim is, perhaps I don't know everyone else's story or how bad some of the victims were abused. As I said earlier, some don't make it through the relationship or maybe paid the price by being in that relationship which may have seemed like forever.

We also develop trust issues which will stay forever when someone takes advantage of us or doesn't live up to their word or if we were tricked or betrayed. I couldn't trust anyone not even someone you loved and if they said they loved you, well that was just words. Don't express your feelings as that just gets you hurt. I grew up in a violent type of family. Funny, I didn't resent my folks though. Perhaps some of the manner in which it showed was skeptical, non-belief and jealousy.

This was how we got to be a victim. You know how to see it through your eyes now try to see it from another perspective and imagine how someone close to you gets tainted or already was or is. If you are able to look at these ideas as though you take each step and stack them on top of each other to determine how much pressure your significant other might be experiencing.

Anger can play an important role; it alerts me and others when I am in distress. It is produced by the fight or flight drug and it may well be the response I developed which causes me to fight instead of fleeing. Who ever heard of a cop running from a call? It is your job to complete the call or mission at whatever it takes. But if we had a difficult beginning or our values and beliefs have been reshaped by our jobs, we might be acting out of the context of adrenalin's true purpose. This where we might try to evaluate the actions we have just been involved within and determine whether this is who we want to be and decide we want to change our life and be a decent person. If we cannot get control of our own life, is it unmanageable?

Anger is meant to be a good thing for us as it helps us prepare for what is next. But it can also be brought out by resentments (which is something we believe was an injustice from long ago) or remembering negative memories. If you can remember something you have not been able to put away, might someone you have been aggressive with be in the boat. I believe anger will eventually turn to rage in time and frustration will be anxiety, which is usually negative thoughts, can trigger anger or rage.

Some might feel trapped by their circumstance (marriage or army) and anger can be how we almost always respond even drunk. It is simply a reaction like our training; we have inadvertently trained ourselves to be this way. Maybe it only worked once but it worked and our minds will keep using it. Unfortunately, we are stuck in a losing game. If you come from an alcohol parent, the other was probably an enabler or maybe an alcoholic as well. That means we do not know what normal is and we will choose a mate like our same-sex parent was; either a drinker or enabler. We think fighting and drinking is a normal way of life and we will probably follow suit and the other events that accompany this sort of upbringing. We don't tell anyone of our family about what is going on as we are ashamed and we are afraid people will think we are not normal. For co-dependence to work in a relationship there has to be like minded person, an aggressor or drinker for the most part and an enabler, one who believes if the abuser (physical, emotional or sexual) didn't drink or beat me or whatever, everything would be fine.

Perhaps you are working at your civilian job and perhaps you overhear some people gossiping or don't approve of their criticism of someone else. You might start to get angry and find you can over react to this. You are a former soldier or cop, you don't walk away. But you find yourself pulled in, perhaps a reaction could also be that you join into the criticism which also stimulates your anger and gets you a reaction in your brain. Maybe you thought this job would just give you some peace as your family is making you crazy. Look at what they made me do! Sorry, the world won't accept this as a reason for you to lose it.

This can be a bigger struggle if you are already having a bad day perhaps things aren't going well or you feel overwhelmed, under-utilized by doing simple work as opposed to what you used to do. Another veteran, big deal, pick something. If you feel trapped into a job, which is nothing like matching your skills, you will feel under-valued (entitled). Having different sorts of negative feelings and being trapped in a job that you need but don't necessarily want will drain your energy, invade your thoughts and keep you stuck. But if some of this makes you feel sick to your stomach or gives you a migraine, what do you do? What if you are a housewife and your spouse is critical of the job you are doing with the kids, the housework, raising the kids on top of the job you do at work, how does that make you feel?

I had many jobs as I would get bored, sometimes, the grass would look greener on the other side (ooh, shiny quarter). I could be very impulsive get bored and create my own entertainment or convince myself to do this or that. I was also easily led at times. You might hear me say some shit about the army, but it was also a place for me where I learned about loyalty, integrity, following a leader, team spirit and how to get people to follow your lead. Stuff, I didn't know about.

I joined the army at twenty-two and spent four years as a soldier. I drank too much only twice and nearly got shot while I was in Cyprus by a Turkish outpost when my buddy got very demanding about getting his cigarette lit. We were in our quarters, which were almost beside a Turkish outpost with three sentries. My buddy couldn't find a lighter or match so, he went outside to the outpost and I followed him trying to keep an eye on him (we were in uniform). He got very agitated when he couldn't get a light for his cigarette and it almost appeared to be drama in action (clown in retrospect). This was about two in the morning. He approached all three sentries individually and was gesturing by pointing at his cigarette hanging out of his mouth but in a very emotional manner. There appeared to be no grasp of our English, but these guys were usually friendly toward us. I wasn't totally surprised when they all stepped back at once. He just persisted but became loud and aggressive. When one of them chambered a round into his sub-machine gun and the others followed suit, I got very calm and stepped back and put up my hands and told my friend Bob (same name) who was standing beside me by now to back up and raise his hands. He continued to rant and rave and I am sure if we'd been armed, there would have been a firefight. I stepped in front of him and stepped into his face and grabbed him and tried to pull him away, they did not lower their weapons, and I got scared. I tried to calm him down and push him out of there backward. He was yelling and swearing and generally making a lot of noise. I was getting him out of there, but now I was concerned the military police were going to show up. I got him back to quarters and calmed him down and got him to bed and sleeping, then I left as my quarters were in another area. He was a real easygoing guy when sober but drunk, he became a lunatic and obviously very toxic and had no idea what he was doing. He was kind of a lonely guy who didn't have much to do with other soldiers or his family or even talk much good about them. Today, I might understand why but this not getting his way must have been some sort of trigger. I wondered if he wanted to die this night. Your spouse probably never got hooked up with the wrong person, not even you?

We start out seeking someone to love and in return that someone will love us. That will work if you are both emotionally mature but if either is from a difficult past or comes back from war with challenges, the relationship can become toxic as well as the other party and the children if there are any.

One scenario is when one of a couple or maybe both start out acting in an appropriate manner to appear more attractive (manipulation is usually learned behavior). Although this behavior is most often seen in men, but I have seen this in women also. We want to be close so we let them in. We weren't listening when they spoke of failed relationships; marriages and we believed they had been some sort of victim. The other person must have been bad, how could they have let this person go. It sounds like the ex was impossible to live with, as now she, or he is impossible to deal with. Maybe this isn't a deal breaker, but who pays attention when in love and that there may be another side to this story. If it sounds good to be true, it probably is.

If there is a sudden onset of behavior change and the other notices, something might be done here but maybe if it has been happening since the beginning, it might not be noticed. I know of married women who have been abused or beaten since dating but always thought it would change or it was their fault or perhaps accepted promises at first. When I was younger and in a relationship, I got into a fight with my girlfriend and she kept putting me down and putting me down and I suddenly lashed out and struck her. I had no idea where this came from, I was so sorry; I couldn't believe I had done such a thing. Obviously the putdowns were a trigger from the past.

By the time you are being verbally abused, the communication has already broken down and you are fearful of what will happen if you speak out or complain. Did the feelings of love already change this quick or were you thinking, it's not that bad. When I speak of abuse, I also speak of emotional, physical or sexual for if your partner isn't happy doing this, it might be a bigger problem.

What usually happens after the first beating, besides forgiveness, is usually PTSD—whether deliberate or unconscious, your mind is burying the incident to try and protect you.

Where are you in the grand scheme of the world? If you have concerns for your safety or that of your children, what are you doing about it? You can be a victim forever and teach your kids to be victims when they grow up. Or maybe you'll become one of those statistics that gets beaten to death. Now that's a tough and painful way to live or die.

Another unfortunate part of this type of relationship is the isolation the battered spouse lives in. They can't let this secret out. What would the world think of me if they saw bruises? That would be embarrassing for the victim and the family. Plus he wouldn't want anyone to know what he is really like. You'll both be onside with the decision to avoid people. Now you can just live in shame and guilt as well, since you are now an enabler. Besides you were never a quitter, better to drink or drug, which you only do to help you cope. No one wants to be alcoholic.

Some might say to leave the abuser. I don't believe it is that easy. Victims have little or no self-esteem after the first few hits and after staying. There is no place to go, the victim must rely on whatever money comes home to feed her and the kids, pay the rent. If you are a responsible person and you have never run away from problems. Now you got no money, you almost live hand to mouth. If you got some drinking issues, your brain may not be clear. So you've got no support, no ideas, and no plan. There may even be pressure from parents, siblings and friends for you to stay. What will people think?

Once communication was really important and once it's gone there isn't much ability to restore it, even if the other is willing to go to counseling and admit to someone what they have been doing to their spouse. I have also seen it where the man doesn't want to change especially if he is abusive, he might not want to give up his slave, his sex slave maybe his punching bag. I don't know of any stories where the spouse/abuser has willingly gone to counseling.

I know of several women (clients) who people believed that they were just a partier and usually got drunk once started. But they would usually get loose morals as the evening drinks flowed. This happened just prior to getting married and early into marriage when her new husband was out of town. They never noticed the change, it was almost like a Jekyll and Hyde thing, and he merely thought she was becoming independent because he was away a lot.

One husband was puzzled as something appeared to be going on and laid awake a lot in bed, had bad dreams, wanted to eat lots when away but avoided her sexually when in town and generally avoiding her and others, preferring to work lots. He had anger from suspicions, coincidental meetings, and gossip but couldn't prove anything. Both are suffering trauma problems which need healing and both may not be willing or aware that their healing is needed, perhaps believing the other is the problem. Getting another person to therapy is very difficult, especially if they don't want to go. Living in denial could mean there is no problem but admitting there is a problem might mean telling the whole truth. You may be motivated to do something but if the other is not, you got nothing. Someone living this sort of relationship may not like it, but perhaps the drinking is to give them peace but, once drunk, they might be looking for someone to just care about them and sex seems right at the time. Sometimes, we confuse with sex with intimacy, thinking that we need sex. Hopefully your partner sees fidelity not as you do?

The typical easy solution we will hear from our family, or friends, is to stand up for ourselves – and that might work if this is your first toxic relationship, or if you come from this sort of life. If this is how you were raised, you don't know if there is any other way to live, as that is all you have ever seen; you don't know what normal is, or what it looks like.

Values and beliefs that we have learned set us up for this. It's unfortunate we don't hire a headhunter to find us a mate as they would probably do a better job of investigating a potential candidate's past. The bigger problem is we will probably repeat this mistake over and over in selection, especially if we drink when we are making a selection about who to drag home for tonight or forever. I must have had a good time; I was laughing and hanging around with others. Sex was good, or at least I wasn't lonely. We believe them and trust them. I know of people who were told by the other that they were a spy, undercover cop, etc. But we trust and accept even their sudden job change as we get to know them and we might be willing to accept them without consideration because, after all, it's not that bad.

If you are one of the lonely people, the need might be more desperate. I don't mean the ones that pretend they got it all together that are starved for affection. How many times do we wait out the relationship before we become intimate – especially if we are getting the high sign? Men are especially gullible on this one. If you aren't one of the beautiful people, you might be so lonely that the first offer is the best one. This might be the one, better not play hard to get.

If you have been hanging around with this person for a while, try to guess how much influence they have over you. And try to decide when you first heard their mild suggestions about how to dress, act, eat, etc. That's okay; they are just trying to be helpful. If you are already holding in the anger and frustration, what do you think this will turn into? Or are you thinking, "If only I could get her/him to change, things would be great." The bad thing about these changes is they create some damage to our self-esteem, especially if attempts at changing you becomes accelerated. This is how the battered wife syndrome begins, and it never stops. She may believe after a while that she is what her husband says; ugly, and stupid. But she can never do enough. If only I did more, tried harder to be better, then maybe the beatings would stop. The change is subtle, she does not notice that much and her typical self-talk might be, "It's not that bad." Most never leave but, if they do, they go back because of promises to change, and because they've got no self-esteem and don't believe they could ever find someone else… or that she couldn't survive without him. The other side of the coin is, are we changing them to be more like us? Then, if they resist, we get more frustrated.

These areas develop without trying. When we get into a fearful situation our brain produces adrenalin. If we constantly live in this state of emotion our anxiety level becomes overactive and we can become hyper-vigilant. What happens if we overuse a drug? Oh well, it wears off and we feel a little down (which is depression). Then we start to need a little more and the "down" goes lower. So, if we get negative, we can get a little more adrenalin, which is followed by a little more depression. It could, and does, become a cycle. Because our system looks for ways to make us feel better, it may come to realize that drinking or drugging might become a good alternative as it provides a little bigger lift than adrenalin. And it can make you feel better but, alas, we start to want a little more, because it will take more and more, or stronger and stronger, to get us "there". Oh yeah, our spouse can get all of this from us, just like we got it from combat. That's right, we came back from combat, knowing how to fight like soldiers, and believing we have also learned to put it away when we get home. Ha. As if!

Chapter Four - Things we can do

I ATTENDED A clinic in the Tacoma and was diagnosed with ADD (ADHD is part of this). This was sort of a relief, as I now knew there was a reason that I am the way I am; I'm not a screw up or a person who deliberately wants to be obtrusive on the world. I began looking at the world in a different manner. I also began taking a supplement called Neuro Link (recommended by Amen Clinics), which fit my particular type of ADD.

I read everything that Daniel Amen wrote about ADD, as well as his programs on healing, how to test people, etc. I almost became obsessive – which is one of my traits that I have been able to use to my advantage. I believed at the time that my whole problem had been my ADHD.

I wanted more out of life and wanted to change, so I decided I wanted help and began seeing a counselor. That was good for about a year, until he took a long holiday. I must have worn him down.

I didn't want to go to therapy because that's for sissies. It wasn't the best way but it got me started on the right path. The hardest thing I ever did was a workbook dealing with fixing me, the second hardest was a counselor who argued with me about what my problems were, or learning how to share at an AA meeting. I might suggest we are too afraid to get in touch with ourselves because of the memories we have buried so deep that we might never find them… nor do we want to. We like to be right and who wants to admit these problems. ADD diagnosis was simple and easily treatable and was easier to admit than being a dry drunk and or crazy.

The replacement counselor I found turned out to be an alcoholism counselor. We couldn't agree on whether I was or I wasn't an alcoholic. I disagreed, and I also believed that ADD played a role in this problem, and that she should treat my ADD. I had read a lot on Adult Children Of Alcoholics (ACOA) and thought that I could be one of them. I went to ALANON for a while (eight months) and it turns out I was ACOA but also a little bit more. I forgot about ADD for a while and joined AA.

The addiction counselor got me into some reading and working a painful workbook. I worked on this workbook every day for months, and I cried every day while doing it, while dredging up painful memories, and I began thinking I was more screwed up than I had previously believed. Therapy is not for sissies. The only good thing about this was I got to be alone. I guess I got to be angry with my past transgressors again, which is better than being bored, which I hate.

A couple of years into AA, I sat down with my friend George, who had been there since I started but never offered me help as I didn't ask. I didn't know he was a counselor who specialized in drunks. I had been like this all my life; never asked anybody for help. Either they saw me struggle and helped me which is drama or I would write them off for not helping me. Perhaps a bit close-minded, because I believed it was all about me. I learned, if we want help, it's like opportunity; we must go looking for help. I told him that I wanted more than not being an alcoholic; I wanted to be free of alcoholism. I didn't want to drink, and I didn't want to be an alcoholic anymore. He started with, "What's stopping you from getting what you want?" I am usually pretty fast with answers, but I was sort of stuck for an honest answer. I have always been a goal or results oriented person and I wanted to get better, but the answer was, I was stopping me. He set me up with a life coach who practiced Neuro Linguistic Programming (NLP), and we worked together for about a year, mostly every two weeks. I learned about how it actually works, and remembered a lot from years ago when I read much about it. I saw how it began healing my trauma and changing my life, and how I was able to let go of some of the old stuff I had hung onto for years without much pain, even though it had been previously painful. While I was working with this coach, she began getting me to attempt some of the exercises on myself and with her as the subject. The more I practiced, the better I got at doing this stuff on myself. I began studying on my own through structured courses.

Fast-forward about a year and George sat me down and took me through one of his workshops. I learned that a person could change their mind and their mood as quick as turning on a dime. I learned to change my mood as quick as I can change my mind. It's funny how you can get help just by asking. I taught myself self-hypnosis and how to gain complete relaxation by taking two deep breaths; focusing on a beautiful picture of a place where I had been and obtaining a full body relax.

I started doing some of the NLP exercises on myself, and found I could change smaller memories or remove them. I practiced self-hypnosis on myself, and found that I could implant ideas into my subconscious (this was really hard). I continued on a learning curve, took more courses, and some included overcoming PTSD. I practiced on friends, family, and strangers at times. I found that I could remove phobias and minor stress related problems in minutes sometimes, and simple things like fear of spiders under a minute. George suggested that I had some sort of skill (some sort of intuition) where I could talk to people easily and they could relate to me. I had told him about a girl who worked as a receptionist at an office I attended. I started a discussion about vacations and she proceeded to tell me how she was afraid of heights, in particular flying and cliffs. While on vacation, she and her boyfriend were on top of a cliff and were supposed to cliff dive. She became somewhat hesitant about diving so her boyfriend just pushed her off the cliff. The next vacation was to include zip lining and she was somewhat reluctant. While I waited for my appointment, we were able to overcome the fear of heights and of flying which she now faced. George suggested I had a lot of nerve and also a lot of confidence to try this with a stranger. She needed help and I helped her.

I began working as a life coach, and found that many people with addictions and stress related problems, including PTSD, seemed to have something in common. They appeared to be very much like me in that we have similar problems with life, with our brains, with our short attention span, with anxiety, depression, impulsive, memory, etc. I began testing for ADD/ADHD with an AMEN Program, and sure enough most people who were coming in had ADD or ADHD. The only ones who didn't were the ones who tested themselves without a family member to mostly confirm their results or the results were even further out of whack than the test subject had stated. It's funny how people like to put their best foot forward. If you ask an alcoholic whether they would rather have ADD or Alcoholism, they choose ADD. I was having extremely good results in healing stress related problems as well as overcoming PTSD.

I continued to do research in this area, which was along the lines of Daniel Amen, and found the Archives of General Psychiatry, which speaks to the issue of a relationship between ADD and ADDICTION. Testing also indicated the levels of depression, anxiety, PTSD, and other symptoms of ADD. A few people sometimes avoid the medical questions about stress related problems, as they could be in denial, or that's stuff they don't want to talk about. People don't like to see themselves as having behavioral problems. Once we can make the determination from testing and knowing their medical background, we can confirm or deny the existence of ADD and the type. The hardest people to change are the ones who don't want to change or give up their obsession or habit, because they are forced by their families through pressure of interventions. They don't want to believe that they have problems. They drink or drug because they just like it, it's a social thing or whatever lie they tell themselves. And we hold onto those awful secrets.

Our typical one on one program might look like this:

1. Learn to relax, and use whenever needed. Provide immediate relief for the client for whatever the person felt was a major issue holding them back (first session).
2. Remove any emotional pain attached to memories from most recent to as far back in the past as needed,
3. Develop strategies for coping, managing, and dealing with stress,
4. Develop goal setting ideas and plans, but first we must be able to see ourselves in the future,
5. Determine and develop an addictive pattern solution for support such as help groups. We also have a need for companionship with like-minded people. If we keep hanging around with the people that were around when we got into trouble, we will keep getting into trouble. One of the problems for many of us was social isolation especially when sober. I believe that working the AA Steps through AA or Alanon can help anyone even non addicts struggling with life.
6. Sometimes keeping a journal of reminders such as these can be invaluable to the right sort of coach or therapist. You saw things that no normal human being has to see, and if you didn't deal with it properly of course it may haunt you.

I have heard of some PTSD sufferers who are able to recover by using simple forms of treatment such as *Eye Movement Desensitization and Reprocessing* (EMDR) or *Eye Movement Integration Therapy* EMIT. We currently use the EMIT technique, but usually in combination with other techniques. I find that this will work well in situations where a person may have gone through situations where he or she may have been exposed to a dire situation and felt nothing but apathy. This is used more as a method of re-attaching the emotion to the picture or memory stored in the mind and being able to conclude the unhappy ending: that is an over-simplified explanation but hopefully you get the gist. I have heard of instances where this treatment works on soldiers who are not ADD or co-dependent and just need help with PTSD.

Try this: close your eyes and visualize the color red and hold it for 30 seconds. Now change it to blue and hold it for 30 seconds. Now change it to yellow and hold it for 30 seconds. Now think of something sad, now picture the color red. Soon as you have red, change it to your favorite color. Think of something that makes you angry, now picture the color red, soon as you have red, change it to your favorite color. Then think of something that frustrates you then picture the color red, then change it to your favorite color. Then think of something that annoys you then picture the color red and continue. This is the basic premise, and if you are seriously disciplined you can do this (soldiers and cops). We teach it in workshops with a lot of prep work. Some people have trouble visualizing colors or anything and it also takes more effort, but anyone can learn to change their mood or getting to a full body relaxation by taking a couple of breaths in any situation by practicing. There are some steps left out, but this is taught in the Dynamic Discovery program, which is a process of self-evaluation, and which is spelled out in my PTSD Workbook.

When we come across people talking negatively, we sort of get drawn into this for a couple of reasons. The negative talk is all about putting others down to make one feel superior. The other is like the news, all about negativity or simply opinions. We hear an opinion about something and it pisses us off and we want to express ours. We get a bit of our adrenalin from either of these methods, which is why we involve ourselves in these types of incidents in the first place. Then we get caught up in who is going to be right, or who is going to win.

You could set yourself some internal guidelines and decide, when you hear this kind of negativity, gossip, or even the news, to immediately walk away and, as soon as you can, picture yourself in the future at a similar situation and picture yourself walking away from a toxic environment before you hear it all and get caught up in it.

Another easy point, I like to stress is the idea of developing an awareness of our behaviors and ourselves. I recommend that a person begin with looking at their surroundings when showering and then paying attention to the water falling upon them, see the surroundings and the soap lather. Feel the water and the washing action of you scrubbing. Listen to the sounds. Allow your body and mind to process all the information at once if possible. Now experience the relaxed feeling you have. Do this and focus on what you are trying to accomplish as a goal (get clean), "To be able to do this without any other thoughts." This will come after some serious practice but extremely valuable.

This is also a good exercise to do while driving, just pay attention to your surroundings, what you see, what you hear and keep your hands on the wheel so you have got something tactile and think about how you feel, mood-wise if you relax. Again consider your destination or objective when driving.

One of the other techniques I use is the idea of praying. I had difficulty with GOD after I lost my children. But once I got started on my road to recovery, I began praying when I would lose it especially while driving. One day within about eight blocks, I had to pull over four times to pray because I was so pissed at other drivers. I later realized, when I get pissed with someone it is more about me being pissed about something in my past life and not so much about what they did but more my reaction. Today, nobody has the right to control how I feel about anything but me. I find the praying works for me and it may work for you. If you are an atheist, you might have to be able to meditate and clear your mind. It's like counting to ten, it gives you a pause to think or rethink your options or just calm down. If you need a twenty count to calm down, take it. This may also be a starting point before we can talk to someone about what bothers us. It just gives us a chance to talk even if it is just to ourselves, we might be able to rethink something stupid we might do. When I think about some of the people I chased, somebody could have been seriously hurt. When I was still a cop, I chased a guy who cut me off and then made faces at me when I was on my way to work. Lucky for him, I was late for work so I didn't stop him. I think, I might have shot him or pounded him, I was so angry. When I first learned how to change colors, I used this a lot to change my rage to calm but I had to practice a lot.

This can be imported by you to anything you do and learn to relax in all you do. This will help you develop an opportunity to pay attention and slow your world down and begin pausing to see and understand about pausing to think before you speak or act.

The point is, do something – I would recommend that you do what I did or see a qualified and experienced NLP Therapist who is familiar with treating PTSD.

Conclusion

WE WERE TRAINED to use our skills to survive and when we are unable to survive in the civilian world what we end up doing is using our military skills to survive. Unfortunately, crime is one of the ways we can survive. If we have killed or been over exposed to violence, our values and beliefs have changed; our old values no longer keep us in check, our new values know no boundaries. Look up the statistics on jailed veterans; or the suicides committed by veterans; and decide whether you want to tough it out or get help. We don't know what normal is anymore, so how can we be normal? We were taught how to how to be soldiers and kill, or whatever our job was, but we were not "untaught" those traits that kept us alive.

We relied on our organization to feed us, shelter us, and provide us with tools to fight with. Our organization made us into tight work units, provided back up resources, provided respite from combat, provided us with leadership on many levels - some actually good. They provided us with a whole bunch of rules to govern our behavior and bound us to obey or suffer imprisonment. All this training and indoctrination will change your values and beliefs. So, we survived, but we don't realize we are survivors; we have become victims of codependence. Now we know how to kill and we will do our job, but the internal conflicts may become great. We were mostly raised to be Christian believers who do things good for the most part. How do you cope with killing, maiming and seeing all that gore after you get to think about it?

We are so screwed up that, at times, we get caught in our own ideas. We form these opinions based on what we think, which may or may not be true. But we could argue black is white and be convinced in our own minds we are right. If someone proves us wrong, well we can just walk away and hate them for the rest of our lives. I can also just get angry and maybe call them out and then they will have to back down. Boy that booze can really help change your thinking at times! It's the same as the news; they report stuff from the enemy side to piss us off with their opinions so we get a bit of adrenalin. I wonder if we get that by bullying people with our stupid opinions.

The other idea I want to entertain here is the oppositional behavior we use to form really quick opinions, or just provide arguments off the top of our heads. We are able to argue black is white, up is down, without any basis for the argument. I say argument because we don't discuss, we argue. This appears one of three ways, either through the ADD personality, addictions, or unfair treatment from an authority figures— where authority figures mean our army training, adults in general when were kids, bosses, teachers, etc. We may have been taken advantage of, mistreated, or unfairly judged. The point is, at some point we decided to fight back and received a dopamine reward as reinforcement, which kept us doing it.

We learn to be highly disciplined because it is so important that we learn to function as part of, and rely upon, our team. We are taught how to be reactive, hyper alert, how to roll with the punches, or bury stuff so we can carry on and do our job. The peer pressure that we have learned to exert on each other to keep us functioning like a machine is all part of the training to keep us under control. We need to control and suppress our feelings, to be tough and do our job until relieved. And, we need to carry away our wounded and dead, especially because they were such a big part of the loyalty and camaraderie we built. We can't snap in the field, because we are needed to protect each other. The battle may be over but we are still in full speed mode. This is another part of the controls built into us from when the training started. They controlled us externally and internally through the training. Our minds didn't know how to come back to our old lives because our beliefs and values were changed by the training, and then the horrors of combat. We couldn't be the same if we wanted to be. We don't fit into the old life. Even though we struggle to fit in, we can't. We try to control everybody and everything around us, including the people in other cars on the roads, in line-ups at the store, the person at the theatre who has his phone on during the movie. If only they would behave or act like us then everything would work out fine. Look at me I'm fine. We hate control now and anyone who tries to control us, but yet we are trying to control everything around us. We are lost but don't know it. We are still soldiers because what we know is to follow the training and you will be okay. We are still there, and definitely not normal.

We come away from this, but because the learning was so good, we can't stop doing it. We keep looking everywhere for enemies or bad guys. Watch a former soldier or off duty cop sit in a restaurant or bar; it will be where they can watch the door and everybody who walks through it. Before they will have sat down, they will have sized everybody up in the place and what they might have to do if there was a problem. Their job was to judge any and all situations to ensure they weren't sabotaged by some "enemy" trying to sneak through lines or into a coffee shop with a bomb. The judging doesn't stop, and we get extremely careful of people even those close to us (hyper-vigilance). We judge everybody mercilessly and we place a label on them, usually something derogatory. I knew of a former soldier who slept with a loaded 9mm and a spare magazine handy in case she ran out of ammo when the second gang of people broke into her house. It was a good neighborhood, so where did the two gangs come from? And why this house? Rational judgment can come into question at times.

To keep ourselves from thinking too much about what we have been exposed to, or what we experienced, many might tell us to keep busy, for a while we are busy doing a job we feel okay. While we are busy, we aren't thinking about the past. The only problem is that many of us turn into workaholics. We again find a way to get some brain chemicals from such activities, and we also understand that other things can help us cope, things such as pharmaceuticals, street drugs, sex, porn, alcohol, etc. Pick something, like going to the gym excessively, or any other thing that can be done obsessively. If we busy ourselves, or delve into distractions, we might be able to bury our pain and memories for long periods of time. We know how to be numb – after all, numb isn't crazy. I did it for about thirty-five years.

I'm just not sure of the mind's need to give us flashbacks. This is the ability to live those horrible scenes over and over every day. It might be for the adrenalin, but it's the mind that decides if it needs a lift, and then it gets it. After all, we might not be crazy, just cunning. Sometimes, in depression or anxiety, a person might flashback; see something, a reminder that triggers us to relive the event. If we get caught in serious depression, we might just lie there or sit somewhere, anywhere - thinking about anything or everything, maybe just become overwhelmed. We can't free ourselves from the memory so it keeps replaying on its own. We become trapped into reliving the memory and forget where we actually are at the time, or who might be with us. We are back in the situation. It also could be like severe anxiety where a reminder has put us back into the anxious situation where we are fighting the battle over again. The bigger problem is, how many times must we fight this dragon? Has anxiety triggered the anger to deal with the enemy? Reaction is a split second, fairly quick. In many situations, if we are unable to debrief at the time of combat or serious situations, we are forced to bury these scenes until later, usually much later.

We are stuck in the past with so many issues. We remember negative emotions such as guilt, which bring the memories back to haunt us, which act as triggers for depression, and both memories and depression keep us stuck in the past and prevent us moving forward. Guilt can be the belief that we wronged someone or some organization at any time in our life and have not been able to put it away.

Our past may have been so painful that it created a stuck point for us. Our ability to mature was halted by the experience. We try to control our lives and dominate and control everyone else's that is around us, believing that if we control how we live and behave that this event will not happen again. That is also anxiety when we fear the future happening the same way it did previously as a kid or a soldier in battle. We have grown up but we still cling to childish ways. Why are we still in the past? That is our life, in the past, it's all we believe we have, we don't know how to live in today much less think of tomorrow.

We don't like to admit we are flawed from our job. What sort of macho soldier or cop would you be if people found out you can't handle it? So, we have the ability to deny there is anything wrong. PTSD is for the guys who couldn't take it. We are really keen on responsibility for anything that might go wrong or did go wrong. We can make excuses for what happened, and many times it might be someone else's fault, or if it wasn't, it should have been as they were a screw up anyway. Here we sit, hoping to be rescued by a great job offer or winning the lottery; not going to happen. We don't do anything to get help because it's not that bad, is it?

The other factor we don't realize is that our brain wants to protect us or make us feel better than we do while suffering. It's a natural reaction to want to find relief from emotional pain. Some do it with prescription medication and others already know that alcohol and recreational drugs can help you get numb. The problem is still there when you wake with a hangover but you got relief for a while. The other problem is that, as we use we develop a tolerance and start needing more and more.

We get into this whole bar culture where we have people we can relate to because that is where the only friends we have hangout. We may need some form of fellowship or camaraderie but this probably isn't the one that is going to do us any good. We even find the opposite sex here. The problem being if they are here for the same reasons we are here for, we just get someone we are attracted to while we are under the influence. I don't know about everybody else, but some of my worst decisions came while I was drunk and in a bar. We associate the bar/liquor to friends, lovers and good times. However, we tend to try and drink later in our drinking lives thinking we will get the good times, companionship, and maybe even lovers. We fail to realize that we are older, and drunks who tend to have big mouths and have little class.

I want to go backwards a bit here. Many of our veterans have been poked and prodded, treated, medicated and sent on their way. One of the things we learned early in life – and from the army – if something doesn't work, stop doing it. So the army doesn't look after you when you get back and Veterans Affairs doesn't help, what are you supposed to do? Keep going? No, I think soldiers get more nervous than they are already. They get gun shy and just stop going. The bigger problem might be that they won't go anywhere because they don't trust anybody. They don't trust psychiatrists, psychologists, social workers, or anyone else in the helping professions. Going to a psychologist can be difficult because a common belief is you have to repeat the memory over and over until you get used to it. Who wants to keep reliving these memories over and over; that's why we are already half nuts.

Whether people see themselves as damaged through their childhood, or from being treated badly, there is a good chance that ADD is involved, especially if their parents didn't have the skills to properly parent. Not many people are willing to admit even to themselves, they come from a screwed up family. ADD kids can be a handful; I was one, and I have met many over the years with various kids' programs. For the kids who grew up without coping skills, and all the kids who were abused, what will happen to them once they hit real adult life without these skills?

We all struggle with life, and some of us experience some form of critical incident. Many times, if we have suffered through a difficult childhood, or experience ADD problems, we may lack coping skills. When a critical incident occurs, our emotional intelligence stops maturing. We become trapped at that time like little children in a body and brain that continues to grow without an emotional maturity to guide us through emotional incidents to be able to come out the other side intact. Whatever age we are, and whatever critical incidents occur after that, we will be unable to deal with it appropriately. That could be a reason we practice so much drama, which is viewed many times as immaturity. I suggest, and others within the NLP community suggest, that events begin stacking themselves on top of the last event, and, at some point, they can become intertwined. The last major event that occurred, becomes the critical incident which pushes our soldier into PTSD. He cannot let go because he doesn't know how to do so.

Our behavior can be displayed in many fashions, from major depression, to being non-functional, to becoming lesser versions, and being somewhat able to function. We seek help and we want to be healed, but the current system, like us, is dysfunctional. We keep doing the same things that don't work, but we still expect different results. I have been there, but I was lucky I found healing.

We ADDers are prone to addictive behavior because we lack coping skills. We don't drink or drug for no reason, we drink and drug to help us fit in to life, or because we didn't know how to cope at an early age. It becomes a way to help us cope; we just want to feel better and fit in somewhere. One of the problems with alcohol is that it is an anti-depressant and it lowers your inhibitions (values), especially with extended usage. Lower enough of your values, and guess what you can become?

We can sometimes bury our problems deep. We don't recall our problems, nor do we want to, and we, as helpers (emergency workers or soldiers), have to be careful when we bring these ghosts back to life that we protect our families and those we are working with so as to not endanger them by making them relive these transgressions against them, because it is heartbreaking for them and us to see any more suffering by reliving some past garbage.

Most cops only see the underbelly of the world; scams, rapists, pedophiles, etc. Continually being surrounded by these people, our values become a bit distorted, and we become what our values have become. An old statistic about cops was that eighty percent of their marriages fail. Guess why? Once we become negative, we lose perspective about many things in the world. I forgot what my original purpose was in life, why was I doing these jobs, which was to serve my country, to protect people. When you only see the bad or negative side of life or your job, a person can become jaded. The people become the enemy when you believe that all there is to life is the bad stuff.

From, "The Dynamic Game" (soon to be in print)

Quote. "A fellow by the name of Robert Fritz created the concept called "Structural Dynamics", which details how structural relationships impact behavior in both individuals and organizations. In his book, Path of Least Resistance, he talks about three insights, the first of which is that energy moves where it's easiest for it to go, which is known as the path of least resistance.

Addicts go through their life following the path of least resistance – which is to "use" – just like a river, where the path of the riverbed is the path of least resistance. To change the path of the river it is necessary to change its underlying structure, which is the riverbed. Rather than damming the river, rather than trying to fight the flow of the water, concentrate on the underlying structure of the riverbed. Because your life can be likened to a river, if you change the riverbed of your life, if you change the underlying structure of your life, then the force of your life, the natural force of your life will flow easily into a new pathway that you've created.

Now how do you do it?

Well let's take a look at the oscillating pattern that most addictive behavior falls into. And that's called the rubber band effect.

When we try and fight against an addiction, it's as if you're in a room and on either side of the room is a large rubber band. And each of those rubber bands attached to the opposite walls are pulled and placed over you so that you are gently pulled in opposite directions. But as you begin to move toward one wall, the tension decreases on the wall that you are approaching and increases on the wall that you are moving away from. And as you get closer to one wall, the pressure from the wall we are moving away from continues to increase and increase and increase and as that tension increases you will eventually tire out and be pulled back in the other direction and snap back toward the opposite wall.

In terms of addiction, as you go farther and farther into the addictive experience and your life narrows and your pleasure diminishes because your life is spiraling down, and you begin to see your addictive behavior as a problem, you are going toward that first wall. And as that becomes increasingly more unattractive to you, there is a point at which you will turn and go the other direction and snap back toward the other wall and say, "I'm going to limit my use of that substance, I'm going to get my life back in control, I'm going to somehow deal with the effects of my addiction by trying to treat the symptoms. I'm at the level of trying to fight the fires that are starting in my life based on the abuse and I'm going toward that other wall.

"And the farther that I get toward that other wall, the stronger the tension becomes from the call of the drug or the call of the alcohol, and as my life starts getting back under control or I start having withdrawal symptoms from the drug or maybe there's a delay between the time that I start to repair my life and the effects of the limiting choices that I've been making, and I can't see the immediate benefit and I'm under stress, then the other rubber band takes effect and I jump back in the other direction, back into the addictive behavior." End quote.

I believe people need to make their own decision about whether their problem also includes addiction. It just seems reasonable that people suffering or struggling with their life might resort to self-medicating. We do have books and workbooks, which can help with addiction whether it is to chemicals or obsessive behavior such as controlling or enabling others. I am speaking of dependency and co-dependency whether to chemicals or people and behavior.

For some reason, we have become terrible at making good decisions; we need sobriety or at least to be able to clear out the garbage. Whether it is AA or Alanon, the twelve-step program can work for anybody but we also need like-minded people and some form of camaraderie, it's there. The twelve steps can help you clean out the garbage in your life and learn to take a look at yourself.

One of the comebacks is to learn to be grateful. My start was writing down three things I was grateful for every day for twenty-one days. Then I did five things I was grateful for thirty days (thanks to Goldie Hawn). Yes, it was hard, but I had to change my ways or I would not survive. Some days, I felt pretty crazy.

Now decide what you want for your future, perhaps first of all, overcoming PTSD. Do you want to carry on in this manner or do you want more? If you are still in a relationship, then are you in or out. If you want to be in and so does your mate, make a list of pros and cons to remain together. Start getting out together even if it is just for coffee, learn to be together again and shut up and let your partner talk. You are sick, you think, it's all about you, it isn't. Start to build some guidelines for being together even if it's just to start dating again but what is good (rules) for one must be good for the other.

If you could make a plan for the next five years of what you see yourself doing or accomplishing and try to see yourself doing the things in the future. Try to imagine what you might look like if you could restore your old values and beliefs in the future. Imagine yourself being able to talk out your problems instead of reacting to them. Get help. If you have to do this on your own, download our PTSD Workbook. It will be difficult but so is your life. Do you want difficulty and to suffer or difficulty and to get better?

Why are our soldiers and emergency workers taking their own lives? I believe they have run out of options and no one from the powers that be hears their cries. Write us and tell us your story. We will create pages for soldiers, cops and other emergency workers to tell their stories. If you have been successful in your healing and have a message for others, we will be glad to know of your secret. If you are frustrated and are suffering perhaps we can build a list of contact information of those needing help and those willing to help. Just provide us with names, details of unit and time of service and location, all separate from your story in the event of a need for anonymity. Have a look at our companion workbook, it's not expensive and it may change your life if you work it. It worked for me. We will soon have an on-line program as well.

You showed courage and love of country, hang in there, it will get better. Help is sometimes hard to find but it can be found. Just keep looking. I found it. God Bless.

I hope that you have found this book informative. I would love if you could you leave me a review so that other readers can find it.

Please check out our website there is great information on it.

If you need any further help please contact me at

www.dynamicdiscovery.ca or www.ptsdtrauma.ca

Bibliography

This can be viewed as a reading list, because these are some of the books, which have helped me on my journey.

Adult Children of Alcoholics, Janet Geringer Woititz
The Adventures of Anybody, Richard Bandler
Alcoholics Anonymous, Alcoholics Anonymous World Services Inc.
Anxiety & Phobia Workbook, Edmond Bourne
Archives of General Psychiatry
The Art of War, Sun Tzu
Big Book of NLP, Shlomo Vaknin
Blueprint For Progress, Alanon Family Groups
Building Emotional Intelligence, Linda Lantieri
Business NLP for Dummies, Lynne Cooper
Change Your Brain Change Your Life, Daniel G. Amen
Change Your Mind And Keep The Change, Steve Andreas & Connierae Andreas
Chickenhawk Back In The World Life After Vietnam, Robert Mason
Clinicians Brain Science Toolbox, Daniel G. Amen
Codependents Guide to The Twelve Steps, Melody Beattie
Codependent No More, Melody Beattie
Codependent No More Workbook, Melody Beattie
The Complete ACOA Sourcebook, Janet Geringer Woititz
The Courage To Heal Workbook, Laura Davis
Daybreak Meditations For Women Survivors of Sexual Abuse, Hazeldon Meditations
Dynamic Discovery, George Bissett
Dynamic Discovery Workbook, George Bissett (and many other books)
Frogs into Princes, Richard Bandler and John Grinder (live)
From Survival To Recovery, Alanon
Healing ADD, Daniel Amen (both editions)
The Healing ADD Power Program, Daniel G. Amen

Healing In Hypnosis, Milton H. Erickson
Healing The Child Within, Charles Whitfield
Healing Trauma, Peter A. Levine
Heart of the Mind, Connirae Andreas and Steve Andreas
How Alanon Works, Alanon Family Groups
Hypnotherapy, Dave Elman
Handbook of Hypnotic Suggestions & Metaphors, Hammond D. Corydon
The Intimacy Struggle, Janet Geringer Woititz
It Will Never Happen To Me, Claudia Black
The Language of Letting Go, Melody Beattie (many other books)
Lifeskills for Adult Children, Janet Geringer Woititz
Lincoln The Unknown, Dale Carnegie
Magnificent Mind At Any Age, Daniel G. Amen
Matrix Energetics, Richard Bartlett
Neuro Linguistic Programming Workbook for Dummies, Ready & Burton
NLP Workbook, Joseph O'Connor
The Physics Of Miracles, Richard Bartlett
Preventing Alzheimer's, William Rodman Shankle and Daniel G. Amen
Recovering From The War, Patience Mason
Releasing PTSD: The Client Session (program), Steve Andreas
Richard Bandler's Guide to Trans-formation, How To Harness The Power of Hypnosis To Ignite Effortless and Lasting Change, Richard Bandler
Self Hypnosis for Dummies, Bryant & Mabbutt
The Structure of Magic, Richard Bandler & John Grinder
The Structure of Magic II, Richard Bandler & John Grinder
Struggle for Intimacy, Janet Geringer Woititz
Superself, Charles J. Givens
The Teachings of Don Juan: A Yaqui Way of Knowledge, Carlos Castanada (and many other of his books)
Theraputic Metaphors, David Gordon
Trans-formations: Neuro Linguistic Programming & The Structure of Hypnosis, John Grinder
Twelve Steps Twelve Traditions, Alcoholics Anonymous World Services
Unchain Your Brain (10 steps to breaking the addictions that steal your life), Daniel G. Amen
Working With Emotional Intelligence, Daniel Goldman

Printed in Dunstable, United Kingdom

91230883R00051